MEXICO

TRAVEL GUIDE

The Ultimate Travel Book To Exploring
The Best Of Mexico

Patrick White

Copyright © **Patrick White**

Disclaimer: The information provided in this travel guide is intended for general informational purposes only. While every effort has been made to ensure the accuracy and timeliness of the information, the author(s) and publisher shall not be held responsible for any errors, omissions, or damages arising from the use of this guide.

Trademarks mentioned in this book belong to their respective owners. The use of these trademarks does not imply endorsement, sponsorship, or affiliation with the book.

Table of Contents

Brief History

Mexico, officially known as the United Mexican States, is a country rich in history and cultural legacy. From its ancient civilizations to Spanish colonization and subsequent war for independence, Mexico's past is a tapestry of varied influences that have defined its identity. This detailed account of Mexico's history seeks to offer travelers a deeper understanding of the country they are visiting.

The history of Mexico extends back thousands of years to the ancient Mesoamerican civilizations that existed in the region. One of the most noteworthy civilizations was the Olmec culture, which formed around 1200 BCE and left behind stunning stone heads and exquisite sculptures. They were succeeded by the Maya culture, noted for their superior writing system, architecture, and mathematical expertise. The Maya cities of Chichen Itza and Palenque are major tourist sites today.

In the 14th century, the Aztecs rose to prominence and constructed their city, Tenochtitlan, in the location of present-day Mexico City. The Aztecs developed a huge empire with a sophisticated social structure and a prosperous economy. They built spectacular temples and devised a calendar system that is still utilized by indigenous groups. However, their power was ultimately conquered by Spanish conquistador Hernan Cortes in 1521.

The Spanish conquest was a crucial turning point in Mexican history. The Spanish colonizers imposed their language, religion (Christianity), and cultural customs on the indigenous inhabitants. This period of colonization lasted for approximately 300 years and had a lasting impact on Mexico's social, political, and economic systems. The influence of Spanish architecture may still be visible in colonial cities such as Guanajuato, Puebla, and Oaxaca.

In the early 19th century, Mexico began to battle for independence from Spanish authority. The struggle for independence was led by people such as Miguel Hidalgo and Jose Maria Morelos, who aspired to free Mexico from colonial domination. On September 16, 1810, Hidalgo gave his famous "Cry of Dolores," signaling the commencement of the Mexican War of Independence. After years of battle, Mexico eventually achieved independence in 1821.

The ensuing decades were distinguished by political instability, as Mexico experienced many internal conflicts and overseas interventions. The Mexican-American War (1846-1848) resulted in Mexico ceding a substantial section of its territory to the United States, including present-day California, Texas, and New Mexico. The French intervention in the 1860s resulted in the construction of a short-lived French-backed monarchy, which was eventually destroyed in 1867.

The 20th century brought substantial social and political developments to Mexico. The Mexican Revolution, which began in 1910, intended to solve concerns of land reform, social injustice, and political corruption. The revolution resulted in the formation of a new constitution in 1917, which provided the framework for Mexico's contemporary political structure.

In recent decades, Mexico has experienced several issues, including economic inequality, drug-related violence, and political corruption. However, it has also witnessed moments of economic development and cultural renaissance. Mexico's diverse art, music, gastronomy, and traditions continue to draw travelers from around the world.

As a tourist in Mexico, recognizing the country's rich history provides a deeper appreciation for its cultural legacy. Exploring historical sites, visiting colonial cities, and engaging with local populations can offer significant insights into Mexico's complex past and present. By acknowledging and honoring Mexico's heritage, travelers can contribute to a more meaningful and responsible travel experience.

Geography

Mexico is a diversified and geographically rich country located in the southern section of North America. It spreads across a vast range of latitudes, encompassing a diversity of landscapes, weather, and natural features. From its broad coasts to its towering mountain ranges, Mexico's geography plays a crucial influence in molding its culture, economics, and wildlife.

Mexico's coastline, which stretches for around 9,330 kilometers, is one of the country's most notable geographical features. The Pacific Ocean, the Gulf of Mexico, and the Caribbean Sea all encircle the nation's eastern, western, and southern borders. These beaches provide Mexico with a wealth of natural resources, including fish stocks, oil deposits, and popular tourist destinations like Cancun and Acapulco.

Moving inland, Mexico is characterized by the huge Mexican Plateau, commonly known as the Central Mexican Plateau or the Mesa Central. This highland region occupies a substantial amount of the country's territory and is bordered by mountain ranges. The plateau, with an average elevation of roughly 1,800 meters, encompasses Mexico's metropolis, the capital and largest metropolis of the country. The plateau's lush soils support significant agriculture, making it a crucial agricultural location in Mexico.

To the east of the Mexican Plateau, the Sierra Madre Oriental and Sierra Madre Occidental mountain range extend parallel to the seashore. These mountain ranges are part of the greater Sierra Madre system that stretches over Central and North America. The Sierra Madre Oriental, closer to the Gulf of Mexico, is recognized for its rocky topography and serves as a natural barrier between the coastal lowlands and the interior of Mexico. The Sierra Madre Occidental, on the other hand, extends parallel to the Pacific coast and is home to the Western Sierra Madre pine-oak woods, which contain rich flora and animals.

In the southern section of Mexico sits the Yucatán Peninsula, a limestone plain that separates the Gulf of Mexico from the Caribbean Sea. The peninsula is noted for its magnificent beaches, cenotes (natural sinkholes), and the ancient Mayan ruins of Chichen Itza and Tulum. It also contains the Sian Ka'an Biosphere Reserve, a UNESCO World Heritage site noted for its biodiversity and wetland habitats.

Mexico is prone to several natural disasters due to its geographical location. It resides in a seismically active zone and receives regular earthquakes. Additionally, the country is susceptible to storms, particularly in coastal regions, which can inflict substantial damage and loss of life.

Mexico's geography also contributes to its abundant biodiversity. The country is considered one of the world's mega-diverse nations, having a vast diversity of ecosystems, including deserts, rainforests, mangroves, and coral reefs. Mexico is home to approximately 200,000 recognized species, including numerous unique plants and animals.

Its geography influences its climate, natural resources, and ecosystems, contributing to the country's cultural legacy and economic activity. Understanding Mexico's geography is vital to appreciate the country's beauty, natural risks, and ecological significance.

Tourists Must Know Information Before Visiting

Before starting your journey to Mexico, it is necessary for travelers to be well informed on the country's customs, culture, safety precautions, and critical travel information. Here are some of the must-know information for travelers visiting Mexico:

Travel Documents: Ensure you have a valid passport with at least six months of validity before visiting Mexico. Depending on your nationality, you may additionally require a tourist visa. It is advisable to check the exact criteria ahead.

Safety: Mexico is typically a safe place to visit, but like any vacation, it is vital to take precautions. Research and stay current on travel advisories and avoid locations with high crime rates. Be cautious with your stuff, especially in crowded tourist locations, and utilize trustworthy transportation providers.

Currency and Exchange: The currency in Mexico is the Mexican Peso (MXN). It is advisable to exchange your currency at approved exchange facilities or withdraw pesos from ATMs. Inform your bank about your travel plans to avoid any complications with card transactions.

Language: The official language of Mexico is Spanish. While English is spoken in tourist areas, it is helpful to acquire a few basic Spanish words to improve communication, especially in more isolated places.

Climate. Mexico's climate varies across the country. It is crucial to understand the weather conditions of your specific trip and pack accordingly. Mexico experiences a rainy season from June to October, so plan for potential showers during this time.

Health and immunizations: Ensure you are up-to-date with routine immunizations. Depending on your trip plans and activity, extra vaccines or measures such as those for hepatitis A and typhoid may be recommended. It is wise to consult with a healthcare expert before flying.

Transportation: Mexico has a vast transportation network. Major cities have airports served by international and domestic aircraft. Public transportation choices include buses, cabs, and the Metro system in Mexico City. Research local transportation choices and trusted businesses to guarantee a safe and reliable journey.

Cultural Etiquette: Mexicans are generally kind and sociable individuals. Politeness and respect for local customs are welcomed. It is traditional to greet with a handshake or a gentle hug. Remember to use "por favor" (please) and "gracias" (thank you) in your interactions. Respect cultural conventions, such as removing your shoes before entering someone's home.

Cuisine: Mexican cuisine is known internationally, and eating local delicacies is a must. Tacos, enchiladas, guacamole, and mole are just a few of the many wonderful alternatives offered. Be mindful of street food cleanliness; seek busy vendors with high turnover to lessen the danger of foodborne infections.

Local Customs and Celebrations: Mexicans celebrate many festivals and traditions throughout the year. Familiarize yourself with the local customs, such as Dia de los Muertos (Day of the Dead) or the lively festivities surrounding Christmas and Easter. These cultural activities offer a unique look into Mexican traditions.

Travel Insurance: It is highly recommended to purchase travel insurance that covers medical emergencies, trip cancellations, and lost possessions. Check the policy specifics to ensure it matches your specific needs.

Remember to embrace the rich culture, discover the different landscapes, and savor the cuisine of this enchanting country.

Best Touring Apps and websites

When it comes to experiencing Mexico, there are several touring applications and websites that can considerably enhance your trip experience. Whether you're seeking information on attractions, lodging, transit, or local suggestions, these sites can give helpful tools and insights. Here are some of the top touring apps and websites for Mexico:

TripAdvisor (*www.tripadvisor.com*): TripAdvisor is a popular platform that gives thorough information on hotels, restaurants, attractions, and activities in Mexico. It gives user-generated evaluations and ratings, allowing you to make informed decisions based on the experiences of fellow travelers.

Airbnb (*www.airbnb.com*): Airbnb is a prominent lodging booking service that offers a wide range of possibilities, including apartments, houses, and unique stays in Mexico. It provides an opportunity to engage with local hosts and explore the nation from a more personalized perspective.

Google Maps (*www.google.com/maps*): Google Maps is a vital tool for navigation, whether you're walking, driving, or using public transportation in Mexico. It gives precise maps, instructions, and real-time traffic information, enabling you to explore the country effectively.

VisitMexico (*www.visitmexico.com*): VisitMexico is the official tourism website for Mexico, giving a variety of information about destinations, attractions, events, and travel ideas. It exhibits the country's unique cultural and natural heritage, providing inspiration and information for your vacation.

Mexico Travel (www.mexicotravel.com): Mexico Travel is another extensive website that offers a range of tools for travelers. It includes insights into popular places, sites, tours, and activities, along with practical information on visas, health, and safety.

Rome2rio (www.rome2rio.com): Rome2rio is a great service for arranging your transit routes in Mexico. It includes complete information on flights, trains, buses, and ferries, allowing you to compare options and choose the most convenient and cost-effective routes.

XE Currency Converter (*www.xe.com*): XE Currency Converter is a dependable tool for converting currencies. It helps you grasp the value of the Mexican peso with respect to your native currency, ensuring you have a clear concept of prices and expenses during your trip.

Mexico City Metro Official App *(iOS/Android)*: If you're visiting Mexico City, this official app gives crucial information about the city's huge metro system. It offers maps, timetables, and travel planning, making it easier to explore the capital effectively.

Yucatan Today (*www.yucatantoday.com*): Yucatan Today is a wonderful resource for people exploring the Yucatan Peninsula. The website gives thorough information on sights, cultural events, restaurants, and activities in the region, including major sites like Cancun, Tulum, and Merida.

iOverlander (_www.ioverlander.com_): iOverlander is a must-have app for tourists planning road trips or camping activities in Mexico. It provides a database of safe and dependable camping locations, petrol stations, and other services, along with user-generated evaluations and recommendations.

These are just a few of the many touring apps and websites available for experiencing Mexico. Each platform offers unique features and benefits, catering to different parts of your travel demands. Remember to check user reviews and ratings, as well as official tourism websites, for the most up-to-date and reliable information. With the help of these tools, you can organize an exciting vacation to Mexico and make the most of your time in this vibrant and culturally rich country.

Top Activities

Mexico offers a wide choice of physical outdoor activities for travelers to enjoy. From spectacular natural vistas to colorful cultural events, the country gives countless chances for adventure seekers and wildlife aficionados. Whether you love water activities, hiking, visiting historic sites, or simply immersing yourself in the beauty of nature, Mexico has something to offer everyone. Here are some of the top physical outdoor activities that travelers can enjoy in Mexico:

Snorkeling or Scuba Diving

Snorkeling and scuba diving in Mexico give amazing possibilities to explore the underwater world of the country's beautiful coasts and thriving marine ecosystems. With its crystal-clear seas, abundant wildlife, and countless dive sites,

Mexico is a wonderful destination for water enthusiasts seeking adventure and discovery.

Snorkeling is an activity ideal for all ages and ability levels, making it accessible to both novices and experienced swimmers. It involves swimming near the water's surface while wearing a snorkel mask, allowing you to breathe through a tube extending above the water. Snorkelers can explore shallow reefs, swim alongside colorful fish, and see intriguing marine life without the need for intensive training or specialized equipment.

Mexico's snorkeling destinations are known for their beauty and diversity. One such site is the Great Maya Reef, the world's second-largest barrier reef, running along the eastern coast of the Yucatán Peninsula. Snorkelers can explore spectacular coral formations, encounter marine turtles, and rays, and even swim with gentle whale sharks in certain seasons. Cozumel, an island off the coast of Quintana Roo, is another famous snorkeling hotspot, famed for its exceptional visibility and magnificent marine scenery.

On the other hand, scuba diving gives a more immersive and exhilarating experience for those ready to explore deeper seas. It involves wearing a self-contained underwater breathing apparatus (scuba) that allows divers to breathe compressed air from a tank. Scuba diving involves proper training and certification, ensuring safety and competency in handling equipment, comprehending dive protocols, and managing underwater situations.

Mexico provides a plethora of world-class scuba diving spots ideal for divers of all levels. The Yucatán Peninsula's cenotes, natural sinkholes filled with freshwater, offer a unique diving experience. Descending into these ancient underground rivers uncovers stunning stalactite formations and strange tunnels, creating an ethereal environment. The Socorro Islands in the Pacific Ocean give a spectacular encounter with enormous marine species, including manta rays, dolphins, and humpback whales. The Sea of Cortez, a UNESCO World Heritage Site, shows bright reefs, playful sea lions, and the opportunity to watch the gentle giants of the ocean, such as whale sharks and humpback whales.

Safety is crucial when partaking in snorkeling or scuba diving activities in Mexico. It is vital to find recognized dive operators and instructors who prioritize safety measures, equipment maintenance, and appropriate diving practices. Additionally, it is vital to be aware of potential risks, such as decompression sickness, and stick to standards to limit environmental effects, such as avoiding contact with marine life or disturbing delicate coral reefs.

Both snorkeling and scuba diving in Mexico provides unique interactions with nature's beauties. The vivid hues of the coral reefs, the exquisite motions of marine life, and the sense of weightlessness underwater provide an awe-inspiring experience. Whether you want to explore the shallow seas with snorkeling or venture deeper into the depths with scuba diving, Mexico's undersea wonders await your discovery.

Hiking

Hiking in Mexico offers a broad range of scenery and experiences, making it an attractive location for adventure-seeking travelers. From towering mountains to lush rainforests and breathtaking coasts, Mexico has much to offer every sort of hiker.

One of the most recognized hiking sites in Mexico is the Copper Canyon in the state of Chihuahua. This huge canyon system, wider and deeper than the Grand Canyon, delivers spectacular panoramas and arduous excursions. The Urique and Batopilas paths give an opportunity to immerse oneself in the region's indigenous Tarahumara culture while crossing breathtaking landscapes.

Another popular hiking spot is the Sierra Norte in Oaxaca, home to ancient Zapotec settlements. The network of trails here allows tourists to explore traditional communities, see various flora and animals, and observe flowing waterfalls. Experienced hikers can take on the hard trip to the summit of Pico de Orizaba, the highest peak in Mexico, located in the state of Veracruz.

For those seeking seaside beauty, the Yucatan Peninsula presents a unique trekking experience. The Sian Ka'an Biosphere Reserve, a UNESCO World Heritage site, has a vast network of paths that wind through lush mangroves, gorgeous beaches, and ancient Mayan ruins. Hikers can also explore the intriguing cenotes, natural sinkholes filled with crystal-clear water, which offer a refreshing escape from the tropical heat.

It is crucial to place an emphasis on safety before setting out on a hiking excursion in Mexico. Always do your research and pick reliable tour operators, or hire nearby guides who are knowledgeable about the trails and can offer crucial assistance. You should let people know about your hiking plans, carry a map or GPS device, and pack essentials like enough water, sunscreen, insect repellent, a first aid kit, appropriate footwear, and clothing for the terrain and the weather here.

Furthermore, respect for the local culture and ecology is vital. Many hiking paths in Mexico run through indigenous communities or protected areas. It is crucial to be sensitive to local customs, request permission when necessary, and leave no evidence of your presence, taking care to properly dispose of rubbish and refrain from hurting the natural environment.

Mexico's hiking trails give a unique opportunity to engage with the country's rich cultural heritage. Along the route, you may oxperience traditional festivals, local cuisine, and crafts that represent Mexico's vivid diversity. Engaging with local communities and supporting sustainable tourism initiatives can enhance your hiking experience while contributing to the preservation of Mexico's natural and cultural assets.

It is worth mentioning that weather conditions might vary greatly depending on the place and time of year. Research the ideal time to visit specific hiking destinations, as some paths may be impassable or risky during certain seasons. Additionally, assess the level of difficulty and duration of the hikes you plan to perform, ensuring they correlate with your fitness level and expertise.

Surfing

Mexico provides a myriad of surf places that cater to different skill levels and tastes. The Baja California Peninsula, notably the region near Todos Santos and Ensenada, is recognized for its regular waves and gorgeous surroundings. Additionally, Puerto Escondido on the Pacific Coast is famed for its big and powerful barrels, attracting expert surfers from around the globe. The Riviera Nayarit, located north of Puerto Vallarta, offers a combination of beginner-friendly breakers and more demanding waves appropriate for intermediate surfers.

The greatest time to surf in Mexico primarily depends on the place you plan to visit. The Pacific Coast has its optimum surf season from April to October when big swells caused by tropical storms and hurricanes give great conditions. On the Caribbean side, the surf season spans from November to March, benefiting from the northern hemisphere's winter storms. However, it's crucial to know that weather patterns can vary, and checking local surf reports and predictions is always suggested.

Beyond the waves, Mexico's rich cultural legacy and colorful coastal communities add to the whole surfing experience. Many surf spots in Mexico offer a laid-back, bohemian attitude, with seaside lodgings, lively restaurants, and local art scenes. Towns like Sayulita, Zihuatanejo, and Tulum provide a unique blend of surf culture, exquisite cuisine, and traditional Mexican charm, creating an immersive experience for guests.

While exploring the surf scene in Mexico, it is vital to emphasize safety. Familiarize yourself with the local surf conditions and the individual hazards of each place. Some breakers have powerful currents, rocky bottoms, or shallow reefs, forcing surfers to exercise caution and find acceptable surf places for their skill level. It is also encouraged to surf with a buddy and obey the local surfing etiquette to ensure a happy and safe experience for everyone.

For novices or those wishing to enhance their skills, Mexico has various surf schools and competent teachers that can provide training adapted to individual needs. These schools often give equipment rentals, giving vacationers the convenience of trying out surfing without bringing their own gear. Whether you're a novice or an experienced surfer, participating in the local surf community can expand your understanding of the sport and develop friendships with like-minded individuals.

Zip-lining

As a popular tourist activity, it offers guests to view Mexico's diverse scenery from a unique perspective, soaring through the air and experiencing an incredible sensation. With its colorful culture, rich history, and magnificent environment, Mexico provides several zip-lining possibilities that cater to all types of adventurers.

Zip-lining includes going between two points on a suspended cable, driven by gravity. In Mexico, this sport is generally practiced in lush rainforests, scenic canyons, or towering mountain ranges, offering participants with awe-inspiring sights and a sensation of complete freedom. Before beginning a zip-lining experience, guests are normally provided with safety equipment, including a harness, helmet, and gloves, along with extensive instructions on how to negotiate the course securely.

One of the most popular zip-lining sites in Mexico is the Riviera Maya, along the Caribbean coast. Here, travelers may explore the region's lush jungles, historic Mayan ruins, and crystal-clear cenotes. Many zip-line tours in this area involve a combination of zip lines, suspension bridges, and rappelling, creating an immersive experience that shows the majesty of the Yucatan Peninsula's natural beauties.

Another notable zip-lining location is Puerto Vallarta, this region offers a broad choice of zip-line courses, often situated inside the Sierra Madre Mountains. Participants can soar through deep forests, crossing gorges and rivers, while being surrounded by stunning beauty and fauna. Some excursions also incorporate additional activities like ATV rides or swimming in refreshing natural lakes, creating a multi-faceted adventure for travelers.

Mexico's colonial cities offer give unique zip-lining experiences. San Miguel de Allende, located in central Mexico, offers an urban zip-lining experience. Visitors can glide around the old city's streets, enjoying panoramic views of its colorful architecture and cobblestone lanes. This blend of ancient charm and adrenaline-inducing activities makes for an amazing adventure.

Tourists should expect that reputable firms would emphasize their well-being by ensuring all equipment is in good condition, employing skilled guides, and performing extensive safety briefings. It is crucial to hire a licensed and registered tour operator to assure a safe and pleasurable journey.

When arranging a zip-lining vacation in Mexico, there are a few items to consider. Firstly, examine the age and weight requirements imposed by the tour operator, as these can vary. Additionally, verify the level of physical fitness required for the individual course, as some may involve hiking or climbing stairs. It is also advised to bring comfortable clothing and closed-toe shoes, as well as sunscreen, insect repellent, and a reusable water bottle.

Rock Climbing

Rock climbing in Mexico offers a diversified and exhilarating experience for adventure fans. With its gorgeous natural settings, rich climbing history, and a large selection of climbing routes, Mexico has become a popular destination for both local and international climbers. Whether you are a beginner or an expert climber, Mexico provides something for everyone.

Mexico is recognized for its magnificent rock formations, such as El Potrero Chico, which is regarded as one of the best climbing places in the country. Located in Nuevo Leon, this limestone wonderland has towering cliffs and a vast variety of routes suited to all skill levels. The spectacular views and demanding climbs make El Potrero Chico a must-visit location for rock climbers.

Another popular climbing area in Mexico is Jilotepec, located in the State of Mexico. This location is renowned for its volcanic rock formations and offers an assortment of bouldering and sports climbing routes. The distinctive volcanic granite provides good friction and numerous climbing options, making Jilotepec a favorite among local climbers.

The Sierra Gorda in Queretaro is another jewel for climbers in Mexico. This region has a magnificent biosphere reserve with towering limestone walls and lovely vistas. Climbing in the Sierra Gorda offers a blend of classic and sport climbing routes, allowing climbers to enjoy the beauty of the surroundings while challenging their skills on the rocks.

For those seeking a coastal climbing adventure, Mexico has various options to offer. Los Dinamos, located near Mexico City, provides accessible sports climbing routes within lovely pine trees. Additionally, the seaside hamlet of La Huasteca in Monterrey is a delight for climbers, with its limestone walls overlooking lush greenery and waterfalls.

When organizing a climbing vacation to Mexico, it is crucial to determine the optimum time to visit. The best climbing season is during the dry months, from November to April, to avoid the wet season and ensure favorable climbing conditions. However, other locations, like El Potrero Chico, can be climbed year-round because of their arid atmosphere.

Mexico provides a strong climbing community, and climbers can find a choice of lodgings and services near major climbing destinations. From campsites to hostels and hotels, there are options to fit different budgets and preferences. Additionally, local guide services are available for people desiring expert guidance and teaching.

Whale Watching

Mexico's Pacific coast, notably Baja California, is considered one of the top whale-watching places in the world. The region draws numerous whale species, including gray whales, humpback whales, blue whales, and orcas. The optimum season for whale watching in Baja California is during the winter months, from December to April when these majestic creatures travel to the warmer waters of the Baja Peninsula. The waters near Baja California serve as breeding and calving areas for multiple whale species, making it a great place for observing their awe-inspiring activities.

The village of Guerrero Negro, located in the Baja California Sur state, is a popular starting place for whale-watching cruises. Here, tourists can go on boat journeys to the surrounding Ojo de Liebre and San Ignacio lagoons, which are famed for their quantity of gray whales. These docile giants approach the boats closely, enabling guests to view their immense size and even pet them at times. It is a truly amazing encounter that displays the gentle nature and intelligence of these remarkable creatures.

Further south, Banderas Bay near Puerto Vallarta is another fantastic whale-watching spot in Mexico. From mid-December to the end of March, humpback whales come to these warm waters to breed and nurse their young. Tourists can join specialist whale-watching trips, conducted by skilled guides who provide insights into the behavior and biology of humpback whales. Witnessing their acrobatic displays, including breaching and tail slapping, leaves people in awe of their grace and might.

On the other side of Mexico, the Gulf of California, popularly known as the Sea of Cortez, offers outstanding prospects for whale viewing. This UNESCO World Heritage Site is home to an astonishing diversity of marine life, including various whale species. From January to April, tourists can view blue whales, the largest mammals on Earth, as they migrate through these seas. Other species, such as fin whales, sperm whales, and orcas, can also be sighted in the Gulf of California.

To ensure an ethical and sustainable whale-watching experience, it is crucial to find reputed tour operators who emphasize the well-being of the whales and follow set criteria. These principles include maintaining a respectful distance from the whales, avoiding unexpected movements or loud noises, and not interfering with their natural activities. By following these rules, travelers can limit their impact on the marine environment and contribute to the protection of these amazing creatures.

Kayaking or Canoeing

Kayaking and canoeing in Mexico provide travelers with a great opportunity to experience the country's numerous waterways, from breathtaking coasts to fascinating cenotes and dynamic rivers. With its rich biodiversity, cultural heritage, and magnificent natural settings, Mexico is a terrific destination for both novice and seasoned paddlers.

Mexico features an extensive coastline in the Pacific Ocean, the Gulf of Mexico, and the Caribbean Sea, providing many chances for coastal kayaking. From the turquoise waters of the Riviera Maya to the rocky cliffs of Baja California, these coastal destinations offer spectacular beauty, secluded coves, and teeming marine life. Tourists may kayak among sea turtles, dolphins, and tropical fish, and discover stunning coral reefs, mangrove forests, and isolated beaches.

Mexico is also famed for its captivating cenotes. These natural sinkholes, situated mostly in the Yucatán Peninsula, offer a unique freshwater kayaking experience. Crystal-clear waters and fascinating underwater caves provide a surreal environment for paddlers. Cenote exploration allows tourists to view spectacular stalactite formations, encounter curious fish, and immerse themselves in the tranquillity of these magical places.

Mexico's numerous river systems give another fascinating choice for kayaking and canoeing lovers. The country is blessed with multiple rivers that cater to varied skill levels. The Rio Usumacinta in the state of Chiapas offers a demanding experience, characterized by swift currents and deep rainforest surrounds. The Rio Filobobos in Veracruz, on the other hand, delivers a spectacular white-water experience via rapids and cascading waterfalls.

Tourists should wear suitable safety gear, including life jackets and helmets, and have a basic awareness of paddling skills. It is essential to join guided tours or employ skilled local teachers who are familiar with the rivers and can provide excellent instruction.

Apart from the intense physical activity, kayaking and canoeing in Mexico give travelers a range of unique experiences. Nature lovers can explore the UNESCO World Heritage Site of Sian Ka'an Biosphere Reserve in the Riviera Maya, canoeing through its beautiful mangroves and witnessing a diverse array of bird species. History aficionados can kayak through the historic canals of Xochimilco, a UNESCO World Heritage Site near Mexico City, where they can view the ruins of pre-Hispanic agricultural systems and traditional trajinera boats.

Moreover, kayaking and canoeing allow visitors to immerse themselves in Mexican culture. Many local villages provide guided tours that combine paddling with cultural encounters. Travelers can learn about traditional fishing skills, discover ancient Mayan sites accessible only by boat, or indulge in great regional food after an eventful day on the water.

Horseback Riding

Horseback riding in Mexico offers a riveting and exhilarating experience for travelers, allowing them to immerse themselves in the rich culture, stunning scenery, and equestrian traditions of the country. With its diverse geography, historical landmarks, and well-preserved natural beauties, Mexico provides an ideal backdrop for riders of all ability levels to embark on memorable equestrian adventures.

One of the most iconic regions for horseback riding in Mexico is the state of Jalisco. Home to the renowned Mexican charro heritage, Jalisco boasts huge ranches where guests may partake in traditional horseback riding adventures. These excursions often feature competent guides who offer insights into the history of charros and their equestrian techniques.

As tourists saddle up and explore the different landscapes of Mexico, they will discover a plethora of alternatives. From visiting the peaceful beaches of Baja California to riding through the lush rainforests of the Yucatan Peninsula, bikers are exposed to a selection of magnificent scenery that exhibits the country's natural splendor. The historic towns of San Miguel de Allende and Guanajuato also offer enchanting horseback rides along their cobblestone streets, allowing visitors to explore the rich history and architecture while enjoying the rhythmic trot of their steeds.

For those seeking an adventurous horseback riding experience, Mexico's rough mountain ranges are a must-visit. The Copper Canyon is a hard yet rewarding track for riders, where they may view the awe-inspiring depths of the gorges while riding alongside local Tarahumara guides. In the Sierra Madre Occidental of Durango, riders can explore secret waterfalls, lush pine woods, and small indigenous settlements, immersing themselves in the region's colorful cultural history.

Moreover, Mexico offers horseback riding vacations that give rare experiences with nature. In the Riviera Maya, riders can explore the Sian Ka'an Biosphere Reserve, a UNESCO World Heritage site, where they may encounter unique bird species, dolphins, and even manatees as they trot along the pristine coastline. The Monarch Butterfly Biosphere Reserve in Michoacán also delivers a beautiful spectacle as riders through the trees, experiencing the yearly migration of millions of monarch butterflies.

Mexico provides numerous trustworthy tour companies that prioritize the well-being of both riders and horses. These operators ensure that tourists are paired with acceptable horses according to their skill levels, offer necessary safety equipment, and hire competent guides who are familiar with the area and local customs. It is recommended for travelers identify recognized and licensed operators and to learn about their safety standards before embarking on any horseback riding experience.

To truly enjoy horseback riding in Mexico, travelers are asked to preserve the natural surroundings, comply with local norms, and engage in sustainable behaviors. Minimizing the influence on the environment, avoiding littering, and following authorized trails are crucial in preserving pristine landscapes for future generations to enjoy.

Paragliding or Hang Gliding

Paragliding and hang gliding are exhilarating adventure sports that allow individuals to experience the sensation of flying like a bird. In Mexico, these sports have acquired appeal due to the country's various landscapes and pleasant weather conditions.

Paragliding and hang gliding are similar in that both sports involve flight using a lightweight, non-motorized aircraft. However, they differ in terms of equipment and method. Paragliding utilizes a paraglider, which is a flexible, inflated wing, while hang gliding involves a rigid-winged aircraft known as a hang glider.

Mexico provides a wide choice of settings for paragliding and hang gliding, each offering distinct experiences. One of the most popular places is Valle de Bravo, located around two hours west of Mexico City. Valle de Bravo is recognized for its picturesque settings, including mountains, lakes, and woods, making it a perfect destination for both beginners and expert pilots. The thermals and wind conditions in this location are well-suited for paragliding and hang gliding, offering a smooth and fun ride.

Another notable resort is Ixtapa-Zihuatanejo, located on the Pacific coast. This region offers spectacular coastal vistas and mild weather, making it a delightful flying experience. With its large expanses of coastline and consistent sea breezes, Ixtapa-Zihuatanejo attracts both paragliders and hang gliders seeking a combination of coastal beauty and thrilling flights.

Tourists should only partake in these activities with certified and competent instructors or operators. Look for trustworthy institutions or organizations that follow strict safety measures and have a strong track record. The instructors will advise participants on proper equipment usage, flight skills, and safety measures to provide a pleasurable and secure experience.

For beginners, tandem flights are a common option. In a tandem flight, a professional pilot follows the passenger, allowing them to enjoy the excitement of flying without the requirement for prior training or expertise. Tandem flights are a fantastic introduction to paragliding or hang gliding and are commonly accessible at most flying facilities in Mexico.

It's crucial to dress adequately for paragliding or hang gliding. Wear comfortable, weather-appropriate attire that provides the flexibility of mobility. Closed-toe shoes with strong ankle support are recommended. Sunglasses, sunscreen, and a hat are important to defend against the sun's rays.

The optimum period for paragliding and hang gliding in Mexico is often during the dry season, which spans from November to April. During this season, the weather is generally stable with minimal rain and consistent wind patterns. However, it's always essential to check the local weather conditions and talk with instructors or operators before booking a flight.

Stand-up Paddleboarding

Mexico's wide coastline offers various sites for stand-up paddleboarding, each with its own unique appeal. The Baja California Peninsula specifically is well recognized for its SUP chances. Destinations such as La Paz, Cabo San Lucas, and Todos Santos provide tranquil, turquoise waters and gorgeous surroundings, offering an excellent backdrop for paddleboarding. The abundant marine life, including dolphins, sea turtles, and colorful fish, adds to the attractiveness of these locales.

The Yucatan Peninsula also is another favorite SUP location. The magnificent blue waves of the Caribbean Sea provide a breathtaking backdrop for paddleboarding. Destinations like Cancun, Tulum, and Playa del Carmen provide a combination of peaceful lagoons, mangrove forests, and ancient Mayan ruins, allowing paddleboarders to immerse themselves in both natural and cultural treasures.

When it comes to choosing a paddleboard, there are various options accessible in Mexico. Many coastal towns and resorts provide paddle board rentals, allowing guests to quickly access the equipment they require. In addition to classic hard boards, inflatable paddleboards have grown increasingly popular due to their portability and simplicity of transportation. Whether you're a novice or an experienced paddler, there are boards suited to every skill level.

One of the advantages of stand-up paddleboarding is its versatility. While paddleboarding on calm waters is perfect for novices, Mexico also offers thrilling chances for more skilled paddlers. Experienced SUP aficionados can take on the challenge of paddling in the ocean, where they can surf waves and explore secret coves. The Pacific Coast, with its higher swells, is particularly ideal for those seeking a more adventurous paddle-boarding experience.

It is necessary to wear a personal flotation device (PFD) and utilize a leash to stay linked to the board. Weather and water conditions should always be taken into mind, and it is best to paddle with a partner or in groups, especially in unknown locations. Local paddleboarding schools and guides can provide vital insights into safety standards and ensure a great experience.

Mexico offers a plethora of physical outdoor activities that cater to varied interests and tastes. From seeing ancient sites and hiking through stunning landscapes to partaking in water sports and enjoying thrilling adventures, there is no shortage of choices for travelers wanting an active and immersive vacation. Whether you're a nature lover, history buff, or adrenaline addict, Mexico's natural beauty and cultural heritage provide the perfect background for a memorable outdoor adventure.

Please note that availability and accessibility to these activities may vary based on the exact area and local rules. It's always advisable to check with local tour operators and authorities for the most up-to-date information and safety rules.

Dialects and Language

With over 68 recognized indigenous languages and varied regional dialects of Spanish, Mexico presents a beautiful linguistic tapestry for travelers to explore and appreciate.

At the center of Mexico's linguistic landscape is Spanish, which serves as the official language of the country. Mexican Spanish has different regional variants, affected by variables such as geography, history, and indigenous languages. For instance, Northern Mexican Spanish has influences from English and indigenous languages, whereas Yucatecan Spanish displays connections to Mayan languages.

However, the linguistic richness of Mexico extends far beyond Spanish. Indigenous languages hold a prominent part in the country's cultural history. Among the most extensively spoken indigenous languages are Nahuatl, Maya, Zapotec, Mixtec, Otomi, and Tzeltal. These languages are spoken by millions of Mexicans, and many groups fight to conserve and promote their ancient tongues.

Nahuatl, the language of the ancient Aztec civilization, is one of the most significant indigenous languages in Mexico. It is still spoken by a substantial number of people, notably in central Mexico. Nahuatl vocabulary has penetrated Mexican Spanish, giving rise to a vast range of place names, cuisine terminology, and cultural expressions that represent the continuing legacy of the Aztec civilization.

Maya languages, spoken mostly in the Yucatan Peninsula and parts of Chiapas, are another prominent group of indigenous languages in Mexico. Yucatec Maya is the most well-known among these languages and holds a significant place in the identity and cultural practices of the region. Maya ruins, like Chichen Itza and Tulum, are not just architectural marvels but also remains of a rich linguistic tradition.

Zapotec and Mixtec, both related to the Oto-Manguean language family, are popular in the state of Oaxaca. These languages have complicated grammatical structures and are noted for their strong oral traditions. Additionally, the Otomi language, spoken in central Mexico, has a substantial number of speakers and is recognized for its musical tone.

Tourists interested in exploring Mexico's linguistic diversity can experience these languages and dialects in action by engaging with indigenous people. Many indigenous towns and villages provide cultural tourism experiences, where visitors can engage with people, learn about their languages, and participate in traditional rites and festivals.

Furthermore, language enthusiasts may find it intriguing to explore language preservation projects and organizations. These programs attempt to archive, revitalize, and promote indigenous languages, enabling chances to learn and respect the linguistic legacy of Mexico.

From the regional varieties of Spanish to the vivid tapestry of indigenous languages like Nahuatl, Maya, Zapotec, Mixtec, and Otomi, Mexico offers a vast linguistic landscape for travelers to explore. By connecting with local people and partaking in cultural tourism activities, travelers can increase their understanding and enjoyment of Mexico's rich language legacy.

Weather

Mexico is a complex country with varying temperatures and weather patterns due to its large size and physical features. From tropical beaches to high mountain ranges, Mexico offers a range of climatic conditions that draw tourists year-round.

Mexico can be split into six primary regions, each having its own characteristic climate: the Northwest, the Northeast, the Pacific Coast, the Gulf Coast, the Central Highlands, and the Yucatan Peninsula.

Starting with the Northwest region, which encompasses Baja California and Sonora, this area has a desert-like environment. Summers are hot and dry, with temperatures often exceeding 100°F (38°C), but winters are moderate and pleasant.

Moving to the Northeast region, which comprises states such as Coahuila and Nuevo Leon, the climate is also arid and semiarid. Summers are hot, with temperatures reaching similar levels as the Northwest. Winters can be cold, especially in mountainous places, with occasional snowfall.

The Pacific Coast region, ranging from Baja California Sur to Chiapas, boasts a tropical and subtropical climate. It experiences two different seasons: the dry season and the rainy season. The dry season lasts from November to May, giving bright and mild weather, making it a perfect period for beach activities. The rainy season, from June to October, offers warmer temperatures, periodic thunderstorms, and greater humidity.

On the Gulf Coast, including states like Tamaulipas and Veracruz, the climate is humid and subtropical. Summers are hot and rainy, with regular thunderstorms and the potential of hurricanes. Winters are milder but still humid, with temperatures ranging from the 70s to 80s°F (20s to 30s°C).

The Central Highlands, home to Mexico City and other important cities, receive a mild temperature due to the high altitude. Summers are often pleasant and rainy, while winters can be frigid, with temperatures occasionally plunging below freezing at night.

Lastly, the Yucatan Peninsula, encompassing the states of Yucatan, Quintana Roo, and Campeche, has a tropical climate. Summers are hot and humid, with temperatures reaching the upper 90s°F (30s°C) with occasional showers. The region is also prone to hurricanes throughout the hurricane season, which spans from June to November. Winters are milder and more comfortable, making it a popular period for travelers.

It's crucial to note that weather patterns might differ within each location due to local geography, elevation, and proximity to bodies of water. Additionally, Mexico's weather is impacted by the North American Monsoon system, which transports moisture from the Gulf of Mexico and the Pacific Ocean, resulting in higher rainfall throughout the summer months.

When arranging a trip to Mexico, it's vital to consider the weather conditions in the exact place you'll be visiting and the time of year. Some places are better suited for beach activities during the dry season, while others offer milder temperatures for seeing towns and cultural sites. Packing proper clothing, such as lightweight and breathable materials for the hot and humid regions, or thicker layers for higher altitudes or winter excursions, is crucial.

Conclusion

Mexico's weather varies widely across its diverse regions. From the arid deserts of the Northwest to the balmy beaches of the Yucatan Peninsula, travelers can find a climate that meets their preferences throughout the year. By understanding the varied weather patterns and seasons, travelers may make informed decisions about the ideal time to come and ensure a more enjoyable and comfortable vacation in Mexico.

Getting Here

Mexico, a vibrant and culturally diverse country, attracts millions of tourists each year with its magnificent beaches, historical attractions, and great cuisine. If you're considering a vacation to Mexico, it's crucial to understand the numerous transit alternatives and admission procedures.

By Air

The most convenient way to reach Mexico for international travelers is by flying. Mexico has multiple international airports, with Mexico City's Benito Juarez International Airport being the principal gateway. Other significant airports are Cancun International Airport, Guadalajara International Airport, and Monterrey International Airport. Several airlines operate direct flights from major cities across the world to these airports. It's advisable to book your tickets in advance and check the admission requirements, and visa.

By Land

You can enter Mexico via land if you are already in a neighboring country or would rather take a road trip. Mexico has common boundaries with Belize, Guatemala, and the United States. There are numerous points of entry along the US-Mexico border, including San Diego, El Paso, and Laredo. Both the Belize and Guatemala borders are crossed in Chetumal and Ciudad Hidalgo, respectively. Before starting a land expedition, make sure you have the necessary permits and that you are aware of the most recent border restrictions.

Entry Requirements

To enter Mexico as a tourist, you will need a valid passport with at least six months of validity remaining. Citizens from several nations, including the United States, Canada, the United Kingdom, and most European Union countries, do not require a visa for tourist stays of up to 180 days. However, it's vital to check the visa requirements based on your nationality. Additionally, ensure you have a completed immigration form, known as a tourist card or FMM (Forma Migratoria Múltiple), which will be provided either during your trip or at the border.

Transportation throughout Mexico

Once you arrive in Mexico, you have many transportation alternatives to tour the nation. Domestic flights are a fantastic choice for traveling big distances fast. Popular airlines like as Aeroméxico, Volaris, and Interjet connect major cities and tourist sites.

Mexico also boasts a well-developed bus network that offers both inexpensive and convenient travel options. Companies like ADO, ETN, and Primera Plus run buses with several classes, including luxury buses with reclining seats and onboard facilities.

For shorter distances or within cities, taxis, Uber, and other ride-hailing services are readily accessible. It's encouraged to use authorized cab services or Uber for safety and convenience.

Mexico offers a range of transportation alternatives for travelers, including air travel, land crossings, and domestic transit. Remember to check the entry criteria, and have the proper travel documents. With careful planning and preparation, you may enjoy a great journey to Mexico, immersing yourself in its diverse culture, magnificent landscapes, and friendly friendliness.

Top Attractions

Mexico has a vast choice of tourist attractions that cater to varied interests. Whether you are an adventure seeker, a history enthusiast, a nature lover, or a foodie, Mexico provides something for everyone. Here are some popular tourist destinations in Mexico:

Chichen Itza

The Yucatan Peninsula in Mexico's Chichen Itza is one of the most well-known archaeological sites in the world. Chichen Itza was formerly a significant Maya city during the pre-Columbian period. Its name, which means "at the mouth of the well of the Itza," alludes to the Cenote Sagrado, a naturally occurring sinkhole that the Mayans revered. This archaeological site, which is around six square miles in size, features a range of Maya and Toltec-inspired architectural styles.

The highlight of Chichen Itza is the spectacular El Castillo, commonly known as the Temple of Kukulcan. This distinctive pyramid dominates the site and stands as a tribute to the superior architecture and astronomical understanding of the Mayans. El Castillo has four sides, each comprising 91 steps, totaling 364 steps, with the platform on top marking the 365th day of the year. During the spring and fall equinoxes, the play of sunshine and shadows creates a magnificent serpent-like illusion, known as the "serpent effect" or the "descent of Kukulcan."

Besides El Castillo, Chichen Itza is home to several more significant buildings. The Great Ball Court, the largest and most well-preserved ancient ball court in Mesoamerica, stands out with its amazing size and artistic sculptures. Visitors might picture the dramatic sporting events and rituals that formerly took place within its walls. The Temple of the Warriors, embellished with beautifully carved columns and statues, and the Temple of the Jaguar, showing its jaguar themes, are also fascinating constructions worth visiting.

Another outstanding landmark of Chichen Itza is the Observatory, commonly known as El Caracol. This spherical tower with its spiral staircase is considered to have been an astronomical observatory, displaying the Mayans' great knowledge of celestial bodies and their movements. Exploring this site gives visitors an insight into the Mayan perspective of the cosmos.

Chichen Itza gives a unique peek into Mayan culture and history. The site features different instructive plaques and signage, as well as knowledgeable tour guides who may offer in-depth explanations. Visitors can learn about the significance of the different monuments, the Mayan calendar, religious practices, and the civilization's downfall.

To make the best of a visit to Chichen Itza, it is advisable to arrive early in the day to beat the throng and the heat. The site opens at 8:00 am, and it is encouraged to visit it at a leisurely pace, allowing adequate time to appreciate the fine intricacies and historical value. Comfortable footwear, sunscreen, and lots of water are necessary for a pleasurable experience.

It is worth noting that Chichen Itza is a UNESCO World Treasure Site and is preserved as a cultural treasure of humanity. To safeguard the site, various restrictions are in place. Climbing El Castillo is prohibited, although visitors can still see it from the base. Additionally, visitors are no longer allowed to swim in the Cenote Sagrado, but they can watch its natural beauty and value from approved sites.

Tulum

Tulum, located on the eastern coast of the Yucatan Peninsula, Tulum's historical significance lies in its ancient Mayan ruins, which are one of the main attractions for tourists. The ruins, positioned on a cliff overlooking the blue waters of the Caribbean Sea, offer an insight into the rich Mayan culture that once thrived in the vicinity. The most noteworthy construction is El Castillo, a tall pyramid that served as a ceremonial center. Exploring the ruins provides a unique insight into Mayan architecture, art, and religious traditions.

Beyond the ruins, Tulum features a bustling cultural scene. The town itself is a lovely mix of classic Mexican architecture and bohemian attitudes. Visitors can meander through its narrow lanes, lined with colorful buildings, boutiques, and art galleries. The local cuisine is another feature, with various restaurants serving wonderful Mexican specialties and fresh fish. Tulum also holds different cultural events and festivals throughout the year, featuring traditional music, dance, and art.

Of course, Tulum is arguably best known for its stunning beaches. The shoreline is endowed with fluffy white sand and crystal-clear waters, making it an enchanting tropical paradise. Playa Paraiso, the most famous beach in Tulum, lives up to its name with its stunning beauty and quiet environment. Visitors can rest under palm trees, swim in the warm seas, or indulge in water activities like snorkeling or diving to discover the vivid coral reefs.

Beyond the beaches, Tulum offers a myriad of natural attractions. The Sian Ka'an Biosphere Reserve, a UNESCO World Heritage site, is a large protected region that comprises tropical forests, mangroves, and diverse fauna. Exploring this ecological gem allows visitors to observe the region's wildlife up close, including rare bird species, dolphins, manatees, and more.

Tulum also caters to people seeking wellness and relaxation. The town has become a magnet for yoga enthusiasts, with various yoga retreats, studios, and wellness centers offering a range of classes and workshops. Many resorts and hotels in the area promote eco-friendly methods, creating a quiet and sustainable atmosphere for visitors.

In recent years, Tulum has experienced a spike in popularity, leading to various issues including over-tourism and environmental concerns. The flood of tourists has resulted in greater development, spurring efforts to balance tourism with preserving the natural beauty and cultural history of the region. Travelers can help sustainable tourism by respecting the local community, practicing eco-friendly behaviors, and supporting responsible enterprises.

Palenque

Temple of Inscription

Palenque, located in the state of Chiapas is an ancient Mayan city that bears immense historical and cultural significance. With its stunning architecture, lush environs, and intriguing archaeological finds, Palenque is a must-visit location for travelers wishing to immerse themselves in the glories of ancient civilizations.

Nestled amidst the lush rainforests of the Chiapas highlands, Palenque shows the remarkable achievements of the Mayan civilization. The city flourished between the 5th and 8th century AD and served as a political and cultural powerhouse. Today, it stands as a UNESCO World Heritage site, drawing people from around the globe.

One of the beauties of Palenque is its amazing architectural features. The most notable is the Temple of the Inscriptions, a towering pyramid that includes a funeral chamber. The temple takes its name from the hieroglyphic inscriptions found inside, which provide vital insights into Mayan history and culture. Exploring the temple's rooms and rising to the summit afford amazing views of the surrounding area.

Another impressive construction is the Palace, an ornate complex with many courtyards, hallways, and terraces. It exhibits the Mayan ability in architectural design and serves as a monument to their advanced urban planning. The Palace's observation tower gives sweeping panoramas of the site and the jungle beyond, producing a sense of awe and wonder.

The site also boasts numerous more temples, residential complexes, and ceremonial platforms, each with its unique architectural style and purpose. The attention to detail and craftsmanship shown in these temples is incredibly amazing, leaving visitors in awe of the Mayan civilization's architectural prowess.

Palenque is recognized for its rich archaeological treasures. The most renowned discovery is the tomb of the Mayan emperor Pakal the Great. This beautifully adorned tomb gives a wealth of information about Mayan beliefs and burial procedures. The jade burial mask found on Pakal's tomb is a masterwork of Mayan artistry and symbolizes the connection between the living and the holy.

Exploring Palenque's wide network of walkways and trails is an experience in itself. Walking through the historic plazas and courtyards, shrouded by the sounds of the rainforest, immerses tourists in a unique ambiance. The jungle's beautiful vegetation and diverse animals, including howler monkeys and colorful birds, add to the magic of the place.

To get the most out of the Palenque experience, it is advisable to engage a competent guide who can provide insights into the historical and cultural significance of the numerous structures. They can assist uncover the mysteries of the Mayan civilization, revealing information on their religious beliefs, governance, and everyday life.

Visiting Palenque requires appropriate preparation due to the site's remote location and hot, humid atmosphere. Comfortable clothing, sturdy footwear, and insect repellant are necessary. It is also essential to carry a drink, sunscreen, and a hat to stay hydrated and protected from the sun.

Teotihuacan

Teotihuacan, located just outside of Mexico City, is an ancient Mesoamerican city that possesses important historical and cultural values. It is a UNESCO World Heritage site and remains one of the most popular tourist destinations in Mexico. Spanning over a wide region of about 20 square kilometers, Teotihuacan provides tourists with a thorough investigation of its remarkable archaeological complex, pyramids, and rich cultural history.

Teotihuacan's beginnings trace back to roughly 200 BCE when the city was initially built. It reached its pinnacle between 150 and 450 CE, becoming one of the biggest towns in the pre-Columbian Americas. The city was a significant hub of trade, religion, and art, influencing the surrounding regions for ages. It was home to a diversified population that prospered under a well-organized social and political structure.

The most renowned constructions at Teotihuacan are its enormous pyramids, the Pyramid of the Sun, and the Pyramid of the Moon. The Pyramid of the Sun, the third-largest pyramid in the world, is a towering edifice that affords an awe-inspiring perspective of the entire complex from its summit. Climbing the pyramid may be a physically challenging yet rewarding experience. The Pyramid of the Moon, located at the northern end of the Avenue of the Dead, gives another breathtaking vista and is a tribute to the city's architectural prowess.

The Avenue of the Dead is the major street of Teotihuacan and runs for about 2.5 kilometers. Lined by smaller pyramids, palaces, and platforms, it provides a look into the city's urban plan and ceremonial significance. The Calzada de los Muertos, as it is called in Spanish, was named by the Aztecs who regarded it to be a sacred spot related to death and the hereafter.

Exploring Teotihuacan also requires visiting the numerous residential complexes and temples found throughout the site. The Ciudadela, a huge courtyard encircled by multiple temples, houses the Temple of the Feathered Serpent (also known as the Temple of Quetzalcoatl). Adorned with complex carvings of serpents and feathered motifs, it offers a prominent example of Teotihuacan's aesthetic and religious expression.

Artifacts recovered at Teotihuacan give light on the city's cultural customs. The site is notable for its mural paintings that show all elements of life, including religious rites, deities, and everyday activities. The Museum of Teotihuacan Culture, located near the archaeological site, gives a thorough display of these items and offers further insights into the civilization that once thrived there.

To enhance the visitor experience, there are guides available who can provide historical and cultural context to the remains. These educated guides may assist travelers appreciate the significance of the monuments, analyze the elaborate murals, and learn about the daily lives of the Teotihuacanos. Additionally, there are audio guides and explanatory signs around the site, allowing guests to explore at their own speed.

In terms of practical considerations, it is important to wear comfortable shoes and clothing suitable for walking and climbing. Sunscreen, caps, and plenty of water are needed, as the Mexican environment may be hot and dry. It is advisable to arrive early in the day to avoid crowds and make the most of the experience.

Cancun

Hard Rock Hotel

Cancun, located on the northeastern coast of the Yucatan Peninsula is a world-renowned tourist resort that offers a complete vacation experience. With its magnificent beaches, crystal-clear turquoise waters, ancient Mayan ruins, exciting nightlife, and opulent resorts, Cancun attracts millions of visitors each year.

Cancun is noted for its stunning white sandy beaches that spread for miles along the Caribbean Sea. The turquoise seas are not only gorgeous but also great for swimming, snorkeling, and diving. The Great Mesoamerican Reef, the second-largest coral reef system in the world, is located close to the coast of Cancun, giving unique chances for underwater exploration. Visitors may explore bright coral reefs, swim with colorful tropical fish, and even encounter majestic sea turtles and whale sharks.

Beyond its natural beauty, Cancun is also rich in history and culture. The region was formerly home to the ancient Mayan civilization, and there are various archaeological sites nearby that offer insight into this intriguing past. Chichen Itza, one of the New Seven Wonders of the World, is a must-visit attraction boasting the renowned El Castillo pyramid. Tulum, another prominent Mayan ruin, offers a spectacular view of ancient temples set on a cliff overlooking the Caribbean Sea.

Cancun's bustling nightlife is another big attraction for travelers. The Hotel Zone, a tiny strip of land that runs along the coast, is crammed with pubs, nightclubs, and restaurants providing a range of cuisines. Whether you're searching for a quiet seaside dinner or an intense night of dancing, Cancun has something to satisfy every taste. The city also holds renowned music festivals and events throughout the year, bringing top worldwide DJs and performers.

For those seeking adventure, Cancun offers a wealth of activities. From zip-lining under the jungle canopy to diving in cenotes (natural sinkholes) or taking a daring ATV to ride around the Yucatan Peninsula, there is no shortage of adrenaline-pumping thrills. Water sports enthusiasts can enjoy jet skiing, parasailing, or kiteboarding, while those seeking a more quiet experience can embark on a leisurely catamaran tour or indulge in a relaxing spa treatment.

In terms of practical knowledge, Cancun enjoys outstanding tourist infrastructure. The city is served by an international airport with direct flights from major cities across the world. Accommodation options are many, ranging from all-inclusive resorts to boutique hotels and vacation rentals. Transportation within Cancun is convenient, with taxis, buses, and rental automobiles easily available.

Cancun also serves as a gateway to other neighboring sites. The Riviera Maya, located south of Cancun, provides gorgeous beaches, ecological parks, and the famed Xcaret, a natural theme park where visitors may swim in underground rivers and learn about Mayan history. Isla Mujeres, a little island off the coast, is noted for its laid-back environment and magnificent coral reefs.

Mexico City

Metropolitan Cathedral

Mexico City, the dynamic capital of Mexico, offers a rich and diverse cultural experience for travelers. With a population of over 21 million people, it is one of the largest cities in the world, overflowing with history, art, gastronomic pleasures, and a busy urban atmosphere. From ancient Aztec ruins to current architectural masterpieces, Mexico City has plenty to interest every tourist.

One of the city's most distinctive landmarks is the Zocalo, the major square located in the historic center. It is one of the largest squares in the world and is flanked by historic buildings, including the Metropolitan Cathedral and the National Palace. The National Palace includes beautiful murals by renowned Mexican artist Diego Rivera, representing the country's rich history.

For history aficionados, a visit to the Templo Mayor is a must. This archaeological site shows the ruins of the Aztec civilization and offers insight into their ancient rituals and way of life. The nearby Templo Mayor Museum provides a full overview of the Aztec culture with its huge collection of antiquities.

Mexico City is also home to various world-class museums. The National Museum of Anthropology is a rich collection of pre-Columbian artifacts, showcasing the different cultures that lived in Mexico before the advent of the Spanish. The Frida Kahlo Museum, popularly known as the Blue House, offers an insight into the life of the famed Mexican artist, Frida Kahlo. Her artwork, personal possessions, and workshop are maintained within this colorful museum.

Art enthusiasts will appreciate the lively art scene that permeates the city. From contemporary galleries in trendy neighborhoods like Condesa and Roma to the street art that graces the walls of communities like Coyoacan, Mexico City embraces creativity in all its manifestations. The annual Zona Maco art fair attracts collectors and artists from around the world, further solidifying the city's standing as an artistic hotspot.

Culinary delights abound in Mexico City, making it a dream for food aficionados. From street tacos and tamales to premium dining experiences, the city provides a varied spectrum of gastronomic pleasures. Sampling traditional Mexican foods such as mole, chiles en nogada, and pozole is a must. Additionally, the city features a bustling food market culture, with markets like Mercado de San Juan offering a variety of fresh fruit, meats, and unusual spices.

Mexico City's neighborhoods each have their own special charm and character. La Condesa and Roma are recognized for their tree-lined streets, chic bars, and hipster culture. Coyoacan, the birthplace of Frida Kahlo, offers a bohemian environment with colorful houses, attractive plazas, and a bustling cultural scene. Xochimilco, with its famous canals and floating gardens, provides a calm getaway from the hectic city center.

Guanajuato

Guanajuato is a dynamic and culturally diverse location that offers a complete experience for travelers. With its stunning colonial architecture, colorful alleys, underground tunnels, rich history, and bustling festivals, Guanajuato has something to offer to every traveler.

Guanajuato's colonial charm is obvious in its architecture and layout. The city's historic core, a UNESCO World Heritage site, is a maze of small, winding alleyways adorned with colorful buildings. One of the most prominent landmarks is the beautiful Basilica of Our Lady of Guanajuato, a majestic basilica that dominates the skyline. The Teatro Juarez, a large neoclassical theater, is another architectural jewel that accommodates a variety of cultural activities.

One of the remarkable aspects of Guanajuato is its huge network of underground tunnels. Originally designed for flood control, these tunnels now serve as roadways for vehicles, making for an interesting and unexpected viewing experience. Exploring the tunnels allows visitors to explore secret nooks of the city and gets an insight into its technical marvels.

Guanajuato's history is inextricably entwined with the Mexican War of Independence, and its museums and sites offer insights into this critical period. The Alhondiga de Granaditas, a former grain storage building turned museum, features historical items and exhibits relating to the battle. Visitors can also explore the birthplace of famed Mexican artist Diego Rivera at the Museo Casa Diego Rivera.

The city is known for its rich cultural scene, and it holds several major festivals that attract travelers from all over the world. The most notable of these is the International Cervantes Festival, a celebration of Spanish literature and drama. During this festival, the city comes alive with performances, concerts, and art exhibitions. The Festival Internacional de Cine de Guanajuato, a renowned film festival, highlights the best of Mexican and worldwide cinema.

Guanajuato's food is a fascinating mix of traditional Mexican flavors and unique peculiarities. Visitors can indulge in regional cuisine such as enchiladas mineras (miners' enchiladas), and the famed Guanajuato-style tamales. The city is also known for its sweet delights, including cajeta (caramel) and jamoncillo (a form of fudge). Exploring the local markets and street food booths is a must for food connoisseurs.

For practical information, Guanajuato offers a selection of housing options to suit any budget, from boutique hotels to homey guesthouses. The city is easily accessible by air, with the nearest airport being the Del Bajio International Airport, located around 30 kilometers away. Once in Guanajuato, travelers can navigate the tight city center on foot, but taxis and local buses are also available for transportation.

Oaxaca

The capital city of Oaxaca, officially named Oaxaca, is a UNESCO World Heritage site and acts as a base for visiting the region. The city is recognized for its colonial architecture, colorful streets, and bustling marketplaces. The main square, known as the Zocalo, is a perfect starting point to take up the ambiance and explore local sights.

One of the delights of Oaxaca is its gastronomic culture. The region is noted for its wonderful and diverse cuisine, which includes traditional dishes like mole (a rich sauce created with chocolate and spices), tlayudas (a sort of wide tortilla topped with various fillings), and mezcal (a distilled alcoholic beverage derived from agave). Food aficionados will pleasure in touring the local markets, trying street food, and dining at traditional restaurants.

Oaxaca is also recognized for its rich arts and crafts culture. The city is home to various art galleries, studios, and artisan markets where tourists may examine and purchase handcrafted pottery, textiles, and other traditional crafts. The surrounding settlements of San Bartolo Coyotepec and Santa Maria Atzompa are famed for their black pottery and green-glazed ceramics, respectively, affording a rare opportunity to observe the artistic process firsthand.

Nature aficionados will find lots to explore in Oaxaca as well. The region features stunning landscapes, notably the Sierra Norte mountain range, which is great for hiking and ecotourism. The Hierve el Agua petrified waterfalls, with their mineral-rich pools and breathtaking views, are a must-visit site. Additionally, Oaxaca's Pacific coastline offers gorgeous beaches and chances for surfing, swimming, and resting.

Another outstanding characteristic of Oaxaca is its indigenous communities and its rich cultural legacy. The Zapotec and Mixtec people maintain a substantial presence in the region, keeping their traditions, dialects, and ceremonies. Visitors can learn about their past civilizations by exploring archaeological sites such as Monte Alban and Mitla, which feature spectacular pyramids and complex stone carvings.

Festivals have a significant role in Oaxacan culture, and travelers should endeavor to experience them during their stay. The Day of the Dead celebrations in late October and early November are particularly famous, with beautiful altars, colorful parades, and excellent food offerings. The Guelaguetza celebration in July exhibits traditional dances, music, and costumes from numerous indigenous tribes, offering a vibrant spectacle of Oaxacan culture.

In terms of practical factors, Oaxaca has a well-developed tourism infrastructure. The city offers a choice of accommodations, from budget-friendly guesthouses to upscale boutique hotels. The local transportation system is reliable and economical, with taxis and buses readily available to tour the city and its surroundings.

Guadalajara

Guadalajara Cathedral

Guadalajara, frequently referred to as the "Pearl of the West," is a dynamic and culturally rich metropolis located in the state of Jalisco. With its intriguing history, gorgeous architecture, lively environment, and wonderful cuisine, Guadalajara offers a complete and unforgettable experience for travelers.

History
Guadalajara has a significant historical significance in Mexico. Founded in 1542, it was one of the first Spanish colonies in the country. The city played a significant role during the Mexican War of Independence in the early 19th century and has since become an important cultural and commercial center.

Architecture

The city boasts a varied spectrum of architectural styles, exhibiting its historical and cultural legacy. The Guadalajara Cathedral, a spectacular specimen of Spanish Baroque architecture, dominates the city's skyline. The Hospicio Cabañas, a UNESCO World Heritage site, is an elegant neoclassical building holding a cultural complex and a notable collection of artwork by José Clemente Orozco. The Teatro Degollado, a stately theater influenced by the neoclassical style, features a variety of shows and is a must-visit for art fans.

Culture

Guadalajara is noted for its robust cultural scene. The city is the cradle of mariachi music, and visitors may immerse themselves in this rich musical legacy by attending exciting mariachi concerts in the Plaza de los Mariachis or exploring the Mariachi Museum. The city is also famed for its traditional Mexican folk dance, known as jarabe tapatío or the Mexican Hat Dance, which is commonly performed at festivals and celebrations. Guadalajara is also home to various museums, including the Regional Museum of Guadalajara and the Museum of Arts of the University of Guadalajara, which display Mexican art and history.

Cuisine

Food aficionados will revel in Guadalajara's food. The city is recognized for its tasty and diversified gastronomic offers. Visitors may experience authentic Mexican cuisine such as birria (slow-cooked pork stew), tortas ahogadas (drowned sandwiches), and pozole (hominy soup). Guadalajara is also the birthplace of tequila, and a visit to the nearby town of Tequila offers the opportunity to explore tequila distilleries and learn about the production process. The city's thriving street food culture is a must-try, with scrumptious tacos, tamales, and elotes (grilled corn) widely accessible.

Events and Festivals

Guadalajara is recognized for its bustling festivals and events throughout the year. The most famous is the International Mariachi Festival, which takes place in September and brings together mariachi bands from all over the world. The Guadalajara International Film Festival, held in March, features a diverse variety of Mexican and international films. The Day of the Dead celebrations in November offers a unique cultural experience, with colorful altars, parades, and customary sacrifices to honor deceased loved ones.

Natural Beauty

While Guadalajara is a bustling urban center, it also gives access to natural beauty. The neighboring Lake Chapala, the largest lake in Mexico, is a popular place for relaxation and outdoor recreation. Visitors can explore the picturesque lakeside towns, enjoy boat trips, or indulge in watersports. Additionally, the Barranca de Oblatos, a magnificent canyon located inside the municipal borders, provides chances for hiking and enjoying nature.

Merida

Merida, the dynamic capital city of the Yucatan Peninsula as well, is a popular destination for travelers wanting a rich cultural experience paired with natural beauty. With its interesting history, gorgeous architecture, wonderful cuisine, and warm friendliness, Merida offers a comprehensive package for travelers.

Merida's rich history extends back to its establishment in 1542, making it one of the oldest consistently inhabited cities in the Americas. The city features a unique blend of Mayan, Spanish colonial, and contemporary influences, reflected in its architecture, traditions, and local culture. One of the must-visit landmarks is the Plaza Grande, the major area surrounded by historic monuments such as the Cathedral of San Ildefonso and the Palacio de Gobierno. These structures are a testament to the city's colonial heritage and provide an insight into its historical significance.

The city's architecture is a sight to behold, highlighted by colorful facades, huge houses, and beautiful ironwork. Take a stroll down Paseo de Montejo, an avenue studded with exquisite French-inspired houses, previously held by the wealthy sisal barons of the 19th century. These homes today house museums, galleries, and boutique hotels, allowing visitors a chance to immerse themselves in the city's history while appreciating its architectural grandeur.

Merida is also known for its strong cultural scene. The city hosts several festivals and events throughout the year, displaying its artistic past. The International Festival of the Mayan Culture is a highlight, commemorating the region's indigenous traditions through music, dance, and art. Visitors can watch colorful parades, traditional performances, and exhibitions that provide a deeper understanding of the Mayan civilization.

To properly experience Merida's culture, one must tour its local markets. The Mercado Lucas de Gálvez and Mercado Santiago give a sensory overload with their lively ambiance, brilliant colors, and a variety of fresh fruit, spices, and handicrafts. Visitors can try classic Yucatecan delicacies like cochinita pibil (slow-roasted pig) and sopa de lima (lime soup), demonstrating the city's unique culinary heritage inspired by Mayan, Spanish, and Lebanese influences.

Nature aficionados can find lots to explore in the surrounding areas around Merida. The region is home to spectacular cenotes, natural sinkholes with crystal-clear turquoise waters, where visitors can swim, snorkel, or simply gaze at the natural beauty. Nearby ecological reserves, such as Celestun and

Rio Lagartos, provide opportunities for birdwatching and encounters with pink flamingos and other wildlife species.

Merida's warm and inviting residents, known as "Meridanos," contribute to the city's attractiveness. The locals take pleasure in their cultural history and are happy to share it with visitors. The city's friendliness extends to its developing network of boutique hotels, offering comfortable accommodations that range from lovely colonial houses to contemporary design-led settings.

San Miguel de Allende

Parroquia de San Miguel Arcángel

San Miguel de Allende is a beautiful location located in central Mexico that provides a rich cultural heritage, stunning architecture, colorful festivals, and a welcoming attitude. As a renowned tourist location, this lovely city has much to offer to travelers seeking an immersive and memorable experience.

San Miguel de Allende is recognized for its colonial elegance and well-preserved Spanish Baroque architecture. Its historic center, listed as a UNESCO World Heritage site, is a treasure trove of architectural masterpieces. The Parroquia de San Miguel Arcángel, an iconic pink cathedral with neo-Gothic spires, dominates the skyline and serves as the city's symbol. Exploring the city's alleys, tourists will meet small cobblestone pathways, colorful facades, and gorgeous courtyards that give a sense of old-world elegance.

One of the beauties of San Miguel de Allende is its burgeoning art scene. The city has attracted various artists and craftspeople from throughout the world, resulting in a flourishing artistic community. Galleries and studios are distributed around the city, presenting a varied spectrum of artistic expressions. The Instituto Allende, a renowned art school, provides chances for guests to engage in seminars and classes, stimulating creativity and cultural interchange.

Additionally, San Miguel de Allende conducts several festivals and cultural events that commemorate its legacy and traditions. The most important of these is the "Fiesta de San Miguel," a week-long event in honor of the city's patron saint, with parades, fireworks, music, and dance performances. The "Candelaria," a spectacular event held in February, highlights the confluence of indigenous and Catholic traditions with colorful processions and raucous street gatherings. These festivals provide a riveting look into the city's unique cultural tapestry.

Furthermore, the gastronomy of San Miguel de Allende is a gourmet treat. From traditional Mexican cuisine to international fusion, the city offers a multitude of eating alternatives to satisfy all palates. Visitors can indulge in mouth-filling street food such as tacos, tamales, and churros, or relish gourmet delicacies at premium restaurants. The city's marketplaces, such as Mercado Ignacio Ramirez, give a sensory experience with their vivid displays of fresh vegetables, spices, and artisanal products.

For those seeking rest and renewal, San Miguel de Allende provides an assortment of spas and wellness centers. Visitors can engage in peaceful massages, thermal baths, and holistic therapies amidst tranquil settings. The city's natural hot springs, such as La Gruta, offer a therapeutic respite from the hectic streets, allowing guests to unwind and refresh.

Beyond the city limits, the neighboring countryside offers stunning views and chances for outdoor activities. The neighboring El Charco del Ingenio is a botanical park and nature reserve that highlights the region's unique flora and animals. Hiking and horseback riding enthusiasts can explore the lovely hills and valleys surrounding the city, taking in stunning vistas and immersing themselves in the natural beauty of the area.

Cabo San Lucas

The Arch of Cabo San Lucas

Cabo San Lucas is a prominent tourist attraction located at the southern tip of the Baja California Peninsula. It offers a great blend of natural beauty, dynamic nightlife, and a large selection of outdoor activities, making it a full package for travelers seeking leisure, adventure, and enjoyment.

One of the biggest attractions of Cabo San Lucas is its gorgeous coastline. The crystal-clear turquoise waters of the Sea of Cortez meet the massive Pacific Ocean, generating spectacular views and affording ample opportunity for water-based sports. The distinctive landmark of the area is the famed El Arco, a natural rock formation at Land's End that marks the meeting point of the two bodies of water. Visitors can take boat cruises to observe this geological marvel up close, along with exploring the neighboring Lover's Beach and Divorce Beach.

The seas of Cabo San Lucas are renowned for their abundant marine life, making it a paradise for fishing enthusiasts. Deep-sea fishing cruises are widely available, allowing an opportunity to catch a variety of fish such as marlin, dorado, and tuna. The region regularly conducts international fishing contests that attract expert fishermen from around the world.

For those seeking excitement, Cabo San Lucas has various possibilities to get your pulse racing. Scuba diving and snorkeling tours allow guests to discover the lively underwater environment filled with brilliant coral reefs and rare marine animals. Thrill-seekers can try their hand at water sports including jet skiing, parasailing, and kiteboarding. ATV tours, zip-lining, and camel rides across the desert landscapes around Cabo San Lucas offer a distinct viewpoint on the region's natural beauty.

Cabo San Lucas features a busy nightlife scene. The downtown area is studded with pubs, clubs, and restaurants offering a range of entertainment alternatives. The Marina sector is particularly vibrant, with premium establishments, live music venues, and exciting nightclubs that cater to all tastes. Visitors can have a fantastic lunch at a seaside restaurant while watching the sunset, followed by dancing the night away at one of the many vibrant clubs.

Cabo San Lucas also has a reputation as a premium vacation destination. It offers a wide selection of accommodations, from luxurious beachfront resorts to budget-friendly motels and vacation rentals. Many resorts in the area include world-class amenities such as spas, golf courses, and exclusive beach access, assuring a soothing and opulent experience for travelers.

When it comes to cuisine, Cabo San Lucas does not disappoint. The culinary scene is diverse and energetic, with a variety of seafood alternatives. From traditional Mexican cuisine to cosmopolitan cuisines, tourists may savor a wide choice of exquisite dishes made by expert chefs. The marina area is famed for its fresh seafood restaurants, where diners may taste freshly caught fish and shrimp meals.

Cabo San Lucas also offers options for cultural discovery. The city boasts a pleasant downtown area with colorful architecture, local markets, and art galleries showing the work of Mexican artists. Visitors can immerse themselves in the local culture by exploring these sites, mingling with the friendly residents, and experiencing traditional Mexican music and dance performances.

Playa del Carmen

Playa del Carmen, located on the eastern coast of the Yucatan Peninsula, is a bustling and popular tourist resort. With its magnificent beaches, rich cultural legacy, and interesting activities, Playa del Carmen offers a comprehensive package as well for those seeking a tropical getaway.

One of the biggest attractions of Playa del Carmen is its magnificent beaches. The city is blessed with crystal-clear turquoise waters and powdered white sands that spread for kilometers. The most famous beach in Playa del Carmen is the Playa Mamitas, where visitors may relax under the sun, swim in the warm seas, and indulge in numerous water sports activities. Additionally, the beach is bordered by various beach clubs, bars, and restaurants, providing a bustling and colorful ambiance.

Beyond the beaches, Playa del Carmen is also noted for its rich cultural legacy. The city boasts a wonderful combination of Mayan, Mexican, and international influences, which is visible in its architecture, gastronomy, and art. A must-visit site in Playa del Carmen is the famed Fifth Avenue (La Quinta Avenida), a pedestrian-friendly thoroughfare that runs along the ocean. Here, tourists may explore an array of stores, boutiques, galleries, and restaurants, offering a fascinating blend of local handicrafts, worldwide brands, and delectable cuisine.

Playa del Carmen also offers a good location for exploring the region's historic Mayan ruins. Just a short distance away, visitors can see notable archaeological sites such as Tulum and Coba. Coba offers a unique experience with its towering pyramids and the ability to climb to the summit for panoramic vistas of the jungle.

For nature lovers, Playa del Carmen has abundant possibilities to immerse in the region's natural beauty. A popular excursion is visiting the adjacent eco-parks, such as Xcaret and Xel-Ha. These parks offer a combination of natural wonders, cultural exhibitions, and thrilling activities. Visitors can swim in underground rivers, interact with dolphins, explore lush jungles, and learn about the area's flora and animals.

Furthermore, Playa del Carmen is a gateway to the world-famous Mesoamerican Barrier Reef System, the second-largest coral reef as described above. Snorkeling and diving aficionados will be in awe of the abundant marine life and brilliant coral formations that thrive in these waters. There are several diving centers and trips available, catering to different skill levels and interests.

In terms of housing, Playa del Carmen offers a wide selection of options to meet every budget and inclination. From opulent beachside resorts to quaint boutique hotels and budget-friendly hostels, there is something for everyone. Additionally, the city's thriving nightlife scene means that visitors may enjoy live music, dance clubs, and beach parties, adding excitement to their evenings.

Isla Mujeres

Isla Mujeres, meaning "Island of Women" in Spanish, is a scenic island located off the eastern coast of Mexico's Yucatan Peninsula. It is a popular tourist destination noted for its magnificent beaches, crystal-clear turquoise waters, active marine life, and laid-back environment.

With a rich history stretching back to the Mayan culture, Isla Mujeres has been a sacred site and a place of worship for the Mayan goddess of childbirth and medicine, Ixchel. The island was later discovered by Spanish explorers and became a pirate haven during the 17th century. Today, Isla Mujeres perfectly integrates its historical charm with modern conveniences to deliver a memorable experience to guests.

One of the biggest draws of Isla Mujeres is its gorgeous beaches. Playa Norte, located on the northern extremity of the island, is widely recognized as one of the most beautiful beaches in the Caribbean. Its pristine white sands, shallow blue waters, and swaying palm palms provide a paradise-like backdrop. Visitors can sunbathe, swim, snorkel, or simply rest under the shade of a palapa.

Apart from its beaches, Isla Mujeres features other interesting attractions. Punta Sur, the southernmost point of the island, is home to a captivating sculpture park including works by local and international artists. The temple devoted to Ixchel, the Mayan deity, is also located here, affording an insight into the island's ancient past.

For marine enthusiasts, Isla Mujeres is a fantastic getaway. The surrounding waters are filled with marine life, making it a hotspot for snorkeling and scuba diving. The Manchones Reef, located just off the coast, is particularly recognized for its brilliant coral formations and complex marine ecology. Visitors can explore the underwater world, encounter colorful fish, graceful sea turtles, and even have the chance to swim with whale sharks during the yearly migration season.

To thoroughly engage in the local culture, tourists can explore the downtown district of Isla Mujeres. The streets are lined with colorful buildings, boutique shops, art galleries, and restaurants providing excellent Mexican food. From fresh seafood delicacies to traditional Mexican tacos, travelers may indulge in a culinary experience on the island.

Getting about Isla Mujeres is relatively easy. Golf carts are a popular means of transportation, allowing travelers to explore the island at their own speed. Additionally, there are regular boat services linking Isla Mujeres to the mainland, specifically from Cancun. The ferry ride takes roughly 20 minutes, making it a suitable day trip for people staying in Cancun or the Riviera Maya.

In terms of accommodations, Isla Mujeres offers a choice of options to meet different budgets and preferences. From luxury beachfront resorts to quaint boutique hotels and vacation rentals, tourists can choose accommodation that meets their needs. It is advisable to reserve in advance, especially during the busy tourist season.

Sumidero Canyon

The Sumidero Canyon is a spectacular natural wonder found in the state of Chiapas. Spanning around 25 kilometers in length, this beautiful canyon is formed by the Grijalva River as it passes through the steep highlands of the Chiapas Highlands. Visiting the Sumidero Canyon offers tourists a rare opportunity to experience breathtaking landscapes, abundant biodiversity, and insight into Mexico's geological history.

One of the most noteworthy features of the Sumidero Canyon is its high cliffs that climb up to 1,000 meters above the river. The sheer scale of these cliffs offers a dramatic backdrop against the shimmering waters of the river, creating an awe-inspiring picture for tourists. These cliffs are the consequence of millions of years of geological processes, with erosion and tectonic action sculpting the canyon into its current form.

Exploring the Sumidero Canyon can be done by a boat cruise along the Grijalva River. This popular activity allows people to fully immerse themselves in the beauty of the canyon. As the boat glides along the river, tourists are treated to stunning vistas of the towering cliffs, rich greenery, and hidden caverns that dot the canyon walls. The boat guides provide educational commentary, providing intriguing insights about the canyon's history, geology, and the various flora and fauna that make it home.

The Sumidero Canyon is not only a geological marvel but also a shelter for wildlife. The canyon's diverse environment is home to numerous animals, including crocodiles, spider monkeys, iguanas, and a vast diversity of bird species. Birdwatchers will be delighted to observe colorful toucans, herons, and kingfishers among the trees along the canyon. With its numerous habitats, the canyon serves as a vital sanctuary for many rare and migratory species, making it a dream for nature enthusiasts and photographers alike.

As travelers venture deeper into the canyon, they will meet stunning sights such as the Christmas Tree Waterfall. This picturesque waterfall falls down the canyon walls, adding to the already attractive scenery.

Apart from the boat excursion, the Sumidero Canyon provides alternative activities for daring guests. Hiking routes allow tourists to explore the canyon's surroundings on foot, getting a closer look at its unique flora and animals. Some routes lead to viewpoints that offer panoramic perspectives of the canyon, allowing tourists to appreciate its magnificence from a different perspective.

When arranging a visit to the Sumidero Canyon, it is recommended to consider the optimum time to go. The dry season, normally from November to April, gives the most optimal circumstances for touring the canyon, with fewer chances of rainfall and clear skies. However, even during the rainy season, the canyon maintains its beauty, since the precipitation generates temporary waterfalls that stream down the cliffs.

Puebla

Cathedral of Puebla

Puebla, located in central Mexico, is a bustling and culturally rich city that offers a complete package for travelers seeking history, art, gastronomic delights, and natural beauty. With its historic architecture, UNESCO World Heritage sites, and inviting environment, Puebla has become a favorite destination for travelers from throughout the world.

One of the highlights of Puebla is its historical core, which is recognized for its well-preserved colonial structures and scenic streets. The heart of the city is the Zocalo, a vast square bordered with colorful buildings and adorned by a gorgeous cathedral. The Cathedral of Puebla, a masterpiece of Spanish Baroque architecture, is a must-visit destination that shows intricate features and stunning interiors. Walking through the tiny lanes of the old center, visitors may observe the stunning facades of buildings coated in multicolored tiles, known as Talavera. Puebla is famous for its Talavera pottery, and tourists can even visit factories and watch the traditional techniques used to manufacture these stunning pieces.

Another noteworthy landmark in Puebla is the Great Pyramid of Cholula, located just outside the city. Considered the largest pyramid in the world in terms of volume, it is a magnificent archaeological monument that offers insight into the ancient civilizations that once thrived in the region. Climbing to the summit of the pyramid provides visitors with a beautiful view of the surrounding terrain and the picturesque town of Cholula.

Food connoisseurs will find themselves in paradise in Puebla. The city is famed for its culinary traditions and enjoys a rich gourmet past. One of the most famous meals from Puebla is mole poblano, a complicated sauce prepared from a blend of chilies, spices, and chocolate, often served over chicken. This tasty and fragrant dish is a must-try when visiting the city. Other classic foods include chiles en nogada, and cemitas, a delectable sandwich made with a sesame-seed bun and varied fillings. Puebla's dynamic street food scene offers a wide choice of appetizing options, including tacos arabes, and the local staple, chalupas.

Puebla is surrounded by natural beauty. The adjacent Popocatepetl and Iztaccihuatl volcanoes provide spectacular scenery for outdoor enthusiasts. Visitors can engage in hiking adventures, take in beautiful views, or even observe the occasional plume of smoke from the volcanoes' peaks. The surrounding countryside is peppered with lovely towns and villages, such as Cuetzalan and Atlixco, where tourists may experience a more slower pace of life and explore local crafts and traditions.

Puebla also hosts different festivals throughout the year, giving an extra dimension of excitement to any visit. One of the most prominent festivals is Cinco de Mayo, which honors the Mexican army's victory against the French soldiers in 1862. The city comes alive with parades, music, dancing, and fireworks, creating a joyous environment that attracts both locals and tourists.

Bacalar

Bacalar, widely referred to as the "Lagoon of Seven Colors," is a stunning tourist site located in the state of Quintana Roo. Known for its breathtaking natural beauty and rich history, Bacalar gives guests a unique and remarkable experience also.

At the heart of Bacalar sits the mesmerizing Bacalar Lagoon, a vast body of water noted for its bright colors. The lagoon's name is derived from its remarkable colors of blue, ranging from turquoise to deep azure, which comes from the various depths of the water and the white limestone floor. The Lagoon of Seven Colors is a sanctuary for nature aficionados and water lovers, providing infinite options for swimming, snorkeling, kayaking, and boating. Exploring the lagoon's crystal-clear waters and discovering secret cenotes and mangrove woods is an adventure in itself.

Apart from its natural beauty, Bacalar also possesses a rich historical past. The village was formerly a prominent Mayan trading station and played a crucial part in the region's history. Visitors can explore the San Felipe Fort, an ancient military bastion erected in the 18th century to safeguard the town from pirate invasions. The fort gives sweeping views of the lagoon and provides insight into the area's colonial heritage.

Another major sight in Bacalar is the Cenote Azul. This gorgeous natural sinkhole is a must-visit for anybody wanting a soothing plunge in its calm, crystalline waters. Surrounded by rich greenery, the Cenote Azul offers a calm and serene environment, making it a great site for rest and reflection.

Bacalar is also home to various eco-parks and reserves that display the region's biodiversity. The Sian Ka'an Biosphere Reserve, a UNESCO World Heritage Site, is a short distance from Bacalar and offers tourists the option to experience tropical forests, mangroves, and unique species. Birdwatching aficionados will be delighted by the profusion of avian species seen in the area.

For visitors wanting a taste of local culture, Bacalar provides a thriving gastronomic scene. Visitors may experience traditional Mexican cuisine, comprising delicacies such as cochinita pibil, ceviche, and fresh seafood harvested from the lagoon. The town's vibrant market is a terrific spot to try local delicacies and acquire homemade crafts and gifts.

Bacalar's laid-back ambiance and friendly residents make a comfortable environment for travelers. The town boasts a range of hotel alternatives, from luxury resorts to modest guesthouses, ensuring there is something to fit every traveler's preference and budget.

El Tajin

Pyramid of the Niches

El Tajin is an ancient archaeological site found in the state of Veracruz. It is listed as a UNESCO World Heritage site and is one of the most important pre-Columbian archaeological sites in Mesoamerica. With its extraordinary architecture and cultural significance, El Tajin offers travelers a rare opportunity to experience the rich history and creativity of the indigenous people who formerly thrived in the region.

The name "El Tajin" means "thunder" or "lightning" in the Totonac language, which is relevant considering the site's relationship with the Totonac civilization. It flourished during the 9th and 13th centuries AD, and its architectural style is defined by its characteristic stepping pyramids, palaces, and ballcourts.

One of the primary attractions in El Tajin is the Pyramid of the Niches, a remarkable structure featuring 365 niches thought to represent the days of the solar year. The pyramid's architecture shows the Totonac's extensive understanding of astronomy and their religious beliefs. Climbing to the top of the pyramid provides tourists with a panoramic view of the entire site.

Another significant feature of El Tajin is the Ballcourt, which is one of the largest and best-preserved ballcourts in Mesoamerica. This ancient sporting venue demonstrates the importance of the Mesoamerican ballgame and its involvement in religious ceremonies and political events. The beautiful stone sculptures and reliefs on the walls portray numerous scenes relating to the game.

El Tajin also has several more constructions, including the Palace of the Columns, the Temple of the Thunder, and the Plaza of the Columns. Each of these architectural marvels features complex carvings and sculptures, highlighting the artistic skill and cultural value of the Totonac people.

Apart from its architectural wonders, El Tajin is also noted for its peculiar iconography. The site is ornamented with exquisite reliefs and sculptures exhibiting motifs such as the feathered serpent, jaguars, and voladores (flying dancers). These symbols provide insight into the cosmology and mythology of the Totonac civilization and add a particular visual appeal to the site.

When visiting El Tajin, it is preferable to explore the monument with a qualified guide who can provide historical and cultural background. The on-site museum exhibits a comprehensive collection of objects unearthed during archaeological excavations, including ceramics, stone tools, and sculptures. The museum provides a great resource for studying the everyday life, religious activities, and creative traditions of the Totonac people.

El Tajin is not simply a historical landmark but also a living cultural heritage. The Totonac people still occupy the surrounding region and maintain their rich traditions. Visitors to El Tajin may have the opportunity to observe traditional Totonac rites, such as the Voladores celebration, in which actors climb a tall pole and fall while linked to ropes, depicting an ancient agricultural process.

Mexico is a location that contains a plethora of attractions, from ancient ruins and beautiful natural wonders to vibrant towns and mouth delicious cuisine. Whether you desire adventure, cultural immersion, or relaxation on gorgeous beaches, Mexico provides a diverse and captivating experience that will make a lasting impact on any tourist.

These are just a few additional attractions that Mexico has to offer. The country is highly diverse and has several sites worth exploring.

Top Cuisine to Try Out

Mexico is a culinary paradise, offering a vast assortment of delectable and unusual dishes that represent the country's rich gastronomic past. From lively street food to beautiful regional specialties, travelers visiting Mexico have a broad range of dishes to enjoy. Here are some must-try delicacies for travelers in Mexico:

Tacos al Pastor

Tacos al Pastor, a treasured culinary gem of Mexico, offers a delectable blend of flavors and textures that enchant both residents and tourists alike. This renowned meal is a must-try for anybody visiting Mexico, giving a complete sensory experience that highlights the country's rich culinary tradition.

Tacos al Pastor traces their origins to the Lebanese immigrants who migrated to Mexico during the late 19th and early 20th centuries. These Lebanese immigrants brought with them the tradition of roasting marinated meat on a vertical spit, akin to Middle Eastern shawarma. Over time, this technique melded with Mexican ingredients and flavors, resulting in the birth of Tacos al Pastor.

The star ingredient of Tacos al Pastor is thinly sliced pork, marinated in a bright blend of spices and herbs. The traditional marinade often includes achiote, a scarlet paste formed from annatto seeds, as well as a blend of dried chiles, garlic, onions, and numerous aromatic spices. The marinade infuses the meat with a rich, savory flavor and lends a distinctive reddish-orange color.

Once marinated, the pork is put onto a vertical rotisserie called a trompo. The trompo slowly rotates, allowing the meat to cook and produce a crispy, caramelized surface while staying tender and moist on the inside. The vertical spit, evocative of the shawarma or Greek gyro, is a visual spectacle in itself and often draws inquisitive observers.

To serve, the cooked pork is thinly cut right from the trompo, with the meat's delicate and savory layers providing the base of the taco. The customary accompaniments for Tacos al Pastor include small, soft corn tortillas, sliced onions, aromatic cilantro, and a splash of fresh lime juice. Some vendors also offer toppings such as pineapple chunks, which lend a pleasant sweetness that beautifully complements the savory qualities of the meat.

One of the distinctive qualities of Tacos al Pastor is its vivid and robust taste profile. The marinade's spices, paired with the slow-cooked pork, create a balanced blend of smoky, acidic, and somewhat spicy flavors. The soft texture of the flesh, paired with the charred edges, gives a lovely contrast, making each bite a blast of flavor.

When it comes to experiencing Tacos al Pastor in Mexico, street food vendors, and taquerias are the go-to destinations. These lively, casual cafés display the art of taco-making, with professional taqueros deftly constructing the tacos with a flourish. The smells of sizzling meat, the sounds of chopping and sizzling, and the sight of the colorful toppings provide an immersive and realistic dining experience.

Chiles Rellenos

Chiles Rellenos showcases the rich and diverse gastronomic heritage of Mexico. It is a delicious blend of flavors and textures that gives a comprehensive sensory experience for food connoisseurs.

Originating from the state of Puebla, Mexico, Chiles Rellenos has become an iconic dish appreciated throughout the country. The term "Chiles Rellenos" translates to "stuffed peppers" in English, and it properly defines the spirit of this dish. The major component is often poblano peppers, which are noted for their mild to medium heat and distinctive flavor. The peppers are usually roasted to enhance their taste and to make the outer skin simpler to peel.

Once the peppers are peeled and the seeds are removed, they are meticulously stuffed with a variety of fillings. The most frequent filling is a blend of cheese, such as queso fresco or Oaxaca cheese, coupled with herbs and spices. However, alternative varieties may contain picadillo (a blend of ground pork, raisins, and nuts), shellfish, or even vegetarian options such as beans and rice. The stuffed peppers are then dipped in a light batter made from beaten eggs, and they are fried till golden brown.

The result is a gorgeously golden and crispy crust that encases a rich, savory center. Chiles Rellenos are commonly served with a thick tomato-based sauce, which further improves their taste. The sauce is often created with tomatoes, onions, garlic, and various spices, cooked together to create a harmonic blend of tastes. Some varieties of the sauce may feature smoky chipotle peppers or roasted veggies for extra depth.

Chiles Rellenos can be enjoyed as a main course, accompanied by rice and beans, or as part of a bigger meal. The dish is a mainstay in Mexican cuisine and is commonly made for special events and family gatherings. It displays the talent and ingenuity of Mexican cooks, who have perfected the art of mixing simple ingredients into a symphony of flavor.

For travelers visiting Mexico, trying Chiles Rellenos is a must to fully immerse oneself in the country's gastronomic traditions. Its brilliant colors, intense flavors, and soothing textures make it a distinctive and delightful dish. Whether you prefer a gentle cheese filling or a more daring seafood alternative, Chiles Rellenos delivers a pleasant gastronomic excursion that reflects the essence of Mexican cuisine.

Mole Poblano

Mole Poblano is a recognized and tasty dish that maintains a prominent place in Mexican cuisine. With a long history and complex blend of ingredients, this savory sauce has grabbed the hearts and taste buds of locals and tourists alike.

Mole Poblano originates in the city of Puebla, Mexico, and retains a long-standing tradition that stretches back several centuries. The meal is said to have been invented by nuns at the Convent of Santa Rosa in the 17th century, merging aspects of indigenous foods and Spanish influences. The name "mole" is derived from the Nahuatl word "mōlli," meaning sauce or mixture.

Preparation and Key Ingredients
Mole Poblano is a complex sauce prepared from a wide assortment of ingredients, resulting in its peculiar flavor profile. The sauce often incorporates dried chili peppers, such

as ancho, mulato, and pasilla, which produce a rich and smokey taste. Other necessary ingredients are tomatoes, onions, garlic, sesame seeds, almonds, raisins, cinnamon, cloves, black pepper, and tortillas. Some variations of Mole Poblano also incorporate chocolate, which lends a note of bitterness and richness to the sauce.

The creation of Mole Poblano is a labor-intensive procedure that requires roasting and grinding numerous spices, toasting the chili peppers, and boiling the ingredients together for hours to obtain the proper consistency and flavor. The final sauce is rich, and velvety, and has a blend of sweet, savory, and spicy elements that tickle the taste receptors.

Cultural Significance
Mole Poblano possesses tremendous cultural significance in Mexico, especially in the state of Puebla. It is considered a festive dish commonly offered for special occasions, such as weddings, birthdays, and holidays like Cinco de Mayo. Mole Poblano has become a vital part of Mexican culture, showcasing the country's rich culinary legacy.

This meal symbolizes the combination of indigenous and European cuisines, emphasizing Mexico's varied background. Its unique blend of spices and ingredients embodies the diversity and depth of Mexican cuisine, and it serves as a source of national pride. Mole Poblano has garnered international prominence and is considered one of Mexico's most iconic foods.

Serving and Enjoying Mole Poblano
Mole Poblano is often served over meat, most commonly turkey or chicken, and accompanied by rice and warm corn tortillas. The sauce can also be used in numerous other

recipes, such as enchiladas or tamales, boosting their flavors and giving a particular touch.

To truly appreciate the taste of Mole Poblano, it is vital to savoring each bite gently, allowing the delicate combination of spices and ingredients to develop on the palette. The richness of the sauce, paired with the soft meat and the matching side dishes, produces a gourmet experience that is absolutely unique.

In conclusion, Mole Poblano is a culinary treat that symbolizes the rich history, cultural significance, and unique flavors of Mexico. Its sophisticated blend of spices and ingredients makes a sauce that is flavorful, spicy, and gratifying. Whether you are a culinary connoisseur or an inquisitive traveler, seeing the delights of Mole Poblano is a crucial element of enjoying the lively Mexican gastronomy.

Tamales

Tamales are created from masa, a dough primarily derived from corn that is blended with various seasonings, fats (such as lard or vegetable shortening), and broth. The masa mixture is poured onto corn husks, which act as natural wrappers. Fillings are subsequently added, ranging from meats like pork, chicken, or beef, to cheese, beans, or vegetables. The husks are delicately folded and cooked, resulting in tender, delicious tamales.

The process of cooking tamales is generally a community activity, bringing families and friends together. It's not uncommon for generations to pass along beloved family recipes, sustaining cultural traditions. During festive events, such as Christmas or Mexican Independence Day, tamales retain a special place on the table, symbolizing unity and celebration.

Regional variants of tamales add to their diversity and intrigue. In Mexico, different states have their own unique styles. For instance, in Oaxaca, you'll find tamales wrapped in banana leaves, stuffed with items like chicken, mole sauce, or even chocolate. In the Yucatán Peninsula, tamales are known as "pibes" and are cooked in underground pits. These variants illustrate the great range of flavors and techniques across the country.

Tamales have a strong cultural relevance in Mexico. They trace their roots back to pre-Columbian times when they were regarded as sacred dishes. Tamales were offered to the gods during rituals and were widely devoured during big rites and feasts. Today, they remain a vital element of Mexican culture, relished in both ordinary meals and special events.

For travelers visiting Mexico, tasting tamales is a must. They can be found in numerous locations, from street food booths to local markets, and even in upmarket restaurants that put a new touch on the original meal. Exploring different regional versions offers a culinary adventure, letting guests appreciate the diverse flavors and textures of this renowned meal.

Enchiladas

Enchiladas are a popular and tasty Mexican dish that has earned international renown for its bright flavors and range of ways. Enchiladas are essentially wrapped tortillas filled with a variety of ingredients and slathered in a tasty sauce. The tortillas used are often made with corn masa, which is a dough produced from ground maize. These tortillas are lightly fried or baked on a griddle to make them malleable before being filled.

The filling of enchiladas varies across Mexico, but frequent alternatives include shredded chicken, beef, cheese, beans, or a mix of these. The tortillas are rolled around the filling, forming cylinders of pleasure. The rolled tortillas are then placed in a baking dish and coated with a good amount of sauce.

The sauce is a significant component of enchiladas and frequently defines the flavor profile of the dish. Traditional enchilada sauces include red sauce, made from dried chili peppers like ancho or guajillo, and green sauce, produced from tomatillos and green chili peppers. These sauces are often prepared with onions, garlic, and spices to enhance their taste.

Enchiladas may be found throughout Mexico, with each region putting its own distinctive spin on the dish. For example, in the northern areas of Mexico, enchiladas are frequently served with a beef filling and topped with a spicy tomato-based sauce. In central Mexico, the enchiladas are commonly packed with cheese or chicken and drenched in a delicious mole sauce. Coastal regions may have seafood-filled enchiladas, served with a refreshing salsa or a sour citrus-based sauce.

Enchiladas can also be served with a number of accompaniments. Common toppings include shredded lettuce, sliced tomatoes, onions, crema (Mexican sour cream), queso fresco (fresh cheese), and cilantro. These toppings add texture and freshness to the dish, complementing the flavors of the enchiladas.

Enchiladas are not just a culinary treat but also a vital component of Mexican culture and tradition. They are commonly offered during festivities, family gatherings, and religious holidays. Their adaptability allows for creativity and personalization in the kitchen, making them a favored choice for both home-cooked meals and restaurant menus.

Pozole

Pozole is a substantial and savory soup prepared mostly from hominy, which is a huge kernel of corn that has been dried and treated with an alkali solution. The dish is frequently connected with Mexican cuisine, particularly in central and southern sections of the nation, where it is regarded as a portion of treasured comfort food and a staple in festivities and gatherings.

To produce pozole, the dried hominy is soaked and boiled until it turns tender and plump. The broth is normally created from simmering meat, traditionally pork, with added ingredients such as garlic, onion, and other herbs and spices. The result is a rich and fragrant base that creates the essence of the dish. Different locations and families may have their own variations of pozole, including red, white, and green varieties, each characterized by the type of chili pepper used in the broth.

Once the soup is finished, it is decorated with a variety of toppings, allowing for personalization and enriching the whole experience. Common garnishes include shredded lettuce, sliced onions, radishes, avocado slices, and fresh lime juice. Additionally, guests can add condiments such as oregano, crushed chili flakes, and hot sauce according to their desire. These garnishes provide diverse textures, flavors, and colors, adding to the attraction of pozole.

Beyond its wonderful taste, pozole is entrenched in Mexican culture and history. The meal has indigenous roots and was traditionally cooked as part of ritual rites and festive occasions, particularly during the harvest season. Today, it is closely associated with festivals like Mexican Independence Day and Christmas, as well as birthdays and family reunions. The act of gathering around a boiling pot of pozole, sharing tales, and enjoying the meal together, strengthens the sense of community and builds a deep connection to Mexican history.

For tourists, sampling pozole is an opportunity to delve into the heart of Mexican gastronomy and discover authentic flavors. Many local restaurants and street food vendors offer this renowned meal, letting tourists experience the original recipes passed down through generations. Exploring different places within Mexico may uncover distinct regional varieties of pozole, each displaying local ingredients and culinary traditions.

Ceviche

Ceviche is a famous and delicious dish in Mexico that is adored by both residents and tourists. Ceviche is a unique dish that involves marinating raw seafood in citrus juices, such as lime or lemon, coupled with a variety of seasonings and vegetables. This procedure "cooks" the fish, giving it a fresh and tangy flavor that is both refreshing and pleasant.

The main ingredient in Mexican ceviche is often fresh fish or shrimp, however, versions with other seafood like octopus or scallops can also be found. The seafood is sliced into small pieces and then blended with a range of spices that enhance the flavors and textures. Chopped onions, tomatoes, cilantro, and chili peppers are frequent additions that provide a kick of heat and freshness to the dish. The citrus juice not only gives a tart flavor but also helps to tenderize and "cook" the shellfish, rendering it opaque and giving it a solid structure.

Ceviche is commonly served as a refreshing appetizer or snack, especially during the hot summer months when its cooling characteristics are particularly appreciated. It is usually accompanied by crunchy tortilla chips or tostadas, which create a pleasant crunch when dipped into the ceviche. Some varieties of ceviche may also contain avocado, cucumber, or mango to lend a touch of creaminess or sweetness to the dish.

One of the beautiful things about ceviche is its adaptability. Different locations in Mexico have their own unique types and varieties of ceviche, each displaying the native flavors and ingredients. For example, in coastal places like Veracruz, ceviche may add olives, capers, and even a hint of jalapeño for a salty and somewhat spicy flavor. In some locations, tropical fruits like pineapple or coconut may be added, lending a tropical touch to the dish.

When visiting Mexico, it is crucial to eat ceviche from various regions to truly appreciate the diverse flavors and styles. Whether you want it mild or spicy, with fish or shrimp, or with a hint of tropical sweetness, there is a ceviche variety to suit every palate. Additionally, it is worth noting that ceviche is often cooked fresh to request, ensuring that you enjoy the best and most flavorful seafood available.

Guacamole

Guacamole is a delicious and versatile dip made mostly from avocados, along with other ingredients that provide taste and texture. In Mexico, guacamole occupies a unique place in the hearts of people and tourists alike, and it is often consumed as a snack, side dish, or addition to various meals.

The primary ingredient in guacamole is the avocado, a fruit that is native to Mexico and Central America. Avocados are rich in healthy fats, vitamins, and minerals, making them not only delectable but also nutritious. To produce guacamole, ripe avocados are mashed until creamy, creating a smooth basis for the dip.

Apart from avocados, guacamole often incorporates numerous other ingredients that enhance its taste and offer a balance of flavors. Lime juice is widely added to guacamole, not only for its sour taste but also because it helps prevent the avocados from oxidizing and turning brown. The acidity of the lime juice provides a pleasant flavor to the dip.

Another crucial element in guacamole is fresh cilantro. Cilantro, often known as coriander, lends a distinct and aromatic taste to the dip. However, some people have a genetic predisposition that makes cilantro taste soapy to them, therefore it can be eliminated or replaced with other herbs like parsley if desired.

Tomatoes are often incorporated in guacamole, providing a luscious and slightly sour taste. Diced tomatoes give a splash of color and help the overall texture of the dip. Other frequent additions include finely sliced onions, garlic, jalapeño or serrano peppers (for a spicy flavor), and salt to taste. The combination of these components generates a beautiful blend of flavors in guacamole.

The creation of guacamole varies slightly across different regions of Mexico, and personal preferences also impact the recipe. Some variants may include additional ingredients like diced mango, pomegranate seeds, or even crumbled cheese. These variants illustrate the versatility of guacamole, allowing it to be adapted to individual tastes and regional traditions.

Guacamole is not only flexible in terms of its components but also in its usage. It can be enjoyed as a dip with tortilla chips, crudités, or even as a spread in sandwiches and wraps. It pairs well with many Mexican foods, such as tacos, enchiladas, and quesadillas, providing a creamy and savory touch to the meal.

In Mexico, guacamole is firmly established in culinary history and culture. Its origins can be traced back to the Aztecs, who were one of the earliest civilizations to cultivate and use avocados. The word "guacamole" itself is taken from the Nahuatl language, used by the Aztecs, and translates to "avocado sauce."

Today, guacamole has become a beloved dish globally, transcending cultural barriers. It is typically connected with Mexican food and is a staple in Mexican restaurants globally. Tourists visiting Mexico have the opportunity to experience real guacamole, prepared with fresh, locally sourced ingredients that showcase the true flavor of this classic cuisine.

Tostadas

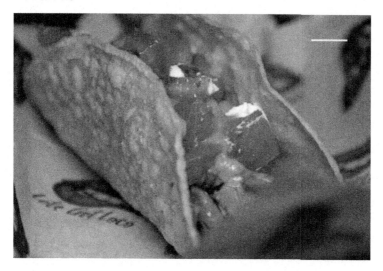

Originating from the pre-Columbian era, tostadas have a lengthy history in Mexican gastronomy. The phrase "tostada" translates to "toasted" in English, alluding to the crispy tortilla base that serves as the foundation for this dish. Traditionally, tostadas were created by deep-frying or toasting tortillas until they become brown and crunchy. Today, commercially available tostada shells are also extensively utilized for convenience.

The production of tostadas begins with the base, a maize or flour tortilla that is either fried or baked until it reaches a crispy quality. The tortilla's thickness varies, and both yellow and white corn tortillas are popular alternatives. Once the tostada shell is done, it becomes a canvas for a plethora of toppings and fillings.

Tostadas offer a limitless assortment of toppings, allowing for a broad spectrum of flavors and textures. Seafood fans can have ceviche tostadas, containing marinated raw fish or shrimp, mixed with lime juice, cilantro, tomatoes, and onions. Alternatively, shredded chicken or beef, refried beans, and various salsas can be utilized to produce robust and delicious tostadas. Guacamole, sour cream, queso fresco (fresh cheese), and pickled jalapeños are traditional garnishes that offer a blast of flavor.

One renowned variation is the Tostada de Tinga, where shredded chicken is cooked in a smokey tomato and chipotle sauce. Another popular choice is Tostada de Pata, which utilizes boiled, seasoned, and shredded cow's foot. These various flavors symbolize the geographical diversity of Mexican food, with each state boasting its own take on the classic tostada.

Tostadas are not only delicious but also offer a visually stunning gastronomic experience. The brilliant colors of fresh ingredients, such as diced tomatoes, sliced avocados, chopped onions, and vibrant salsas, provide a feast for the eyes. Moreover, the mix of crispy tostada shells and liquid toppings gives a delicious sensory contrast.

When visiting Mexico's culinary environment, indulging in tostadas is a must for any traveler seeking an authentic and diverse gourmet experience. Whether consuming them at local street food stands, family-owned restaurants, or fancy establishments, tostadas offer a flavor of Mexico's cultural history. By experiencing the numerous regional interpretations and experimenting with different toppings, travelers may completely immerse themselves in the vivid and tantalizing world of Mexican cuisine.

Sopes

These delightful delights are a fundamental element of Mexican cuisine and offer a unique culinary experience that shows the colorful tastes and various ingredients of the country.

Sopes are a sort of antojito, which translates to "little cravings" in English. They are essentially thick, round maize masa (dough) patties that are somewhat concave in shape. The dough is created from masa harina (a type of corn flour), water, and sometimes a bit of salt. The dough is then flattened by hand into a thick tortilla-like form and baked on a griddle or comal until it gets golden brown and slightly crunchy.

Once the sopes are prepared, they are customarily topped with a variety of ingredients that vary from region to region and even from one street seller to another. Common toppings include refried beans, shredded or sliced meat (such as beef, chicken, or pig), queso fresco (fresh cheese), lettuce, tomatoes, onions, avocado slices, and salsa. The possibilities are unlimited, and half of the pleasure is choosing your favorite toppings or experimenting with other flavors.

Sopes are commonly enjoyed as a snack or appetizer, but they can also be a full dinner on their own. They offer a delicious combination of textures, with the crispy outside of the masa complementing the soft and tasty toppings. The combination of flavors, from the creamy beans to the tangy cheese and spicy salsa, makes a harmonic blend that will excite your taste buds.

One of the best aspects of sopes is their adaptability. They can be adjusted to fit varied dietary choices and constraints. Vegetarians can opt for bean-based fillings and load up on fresh veggies, while meat eaters can indulge in savory selections like shredded chicken or beef. Sopes may be found in street food booths, marketplaces, and restaurants throughout Mexico, and each place adds its own distinctive spin to this favorite delicacy.

Chiles en Nogada

Chiles en Nogada is often connected with the state of Puebla and has become a hallmark of Mexican gastronomy. Chiles en Nogada is often served with poblano peppers, which are mild chili peppers with a unique dark green color. The name "en Nogada" relates to the creamy walnut sauce, known as nogada, that accompanies the dish. This sauce is a key element and plays a crucial function in the overall flavor profile of the dish.

The dish's origins can be traced back to the early 19th century in Puebla, Mexico. It is thought to have been erected by sisters from the Santa Monica convent to honor a visit from Agustín de Iturbide, a Mexican military and political leader who subsequently became the country's emperor. The nuns sought to exhibit the colors of the Mexican flag in a dish, and thus Chiles en Nogada was conceived. The green chili represents independence, the white nogada symbolizes purity, and the red pomegranate seeds signify the bloodshed of those who fought for Mexico's independence.

The preparation of Chiles en Nogada is rigorous and time-consuming. The poblano peppers are roasted, skinned, and then carefully stuffed with a mixture of picadillo, a savory filling often prepared with ground pork, fruits, spices, and herbs. The picadillo is generally created with a combination of ground beef or pig, along with ingredients like onion, garlic, tomatoes, raisins, and almonds, producing a perfect blend of sweet and salty flavors.

Once packed, the chilies are topped with creamy nogada sauce, made from ground walnuts, milk, queso fresco (a soft white cheese), and a hint of sherry. The nogada sauce is delicate, creamy, and somewhat sweet, lending a silky texture to the dish. Finally, the chiles are topped with pomegranate seeds and chopped parsley, creating a burst of color and freshness.

Chiles en Nogada is traditionally served chilled, making it an excellent dish for the warmer months. Its blend of flavors, textures, and colors makes it a veritable feast for the senses. The meal demonstrates the richness and diversity of Mexican cuisine, merging indigenous ingredients with European influences.

As a tourist, experiencing Chiles en Nogada is a culinary experience that allows you to connect with Mexican history and culture. It is commonly served during the patriotic celebrations of Mexican Independence Day in September, but it can be found in restaurants and food vendors throughout the year. Don't miss the opportunity to sample this renowned

Mexican cuisine and appreciate the expertise and artistry that goes into its creation.

Aguachile

Aguachile originated from the coastal regions of Mexico, mainly Sinaloa, and Nayarit. It is a mainstay of Mexican cuisine and a must-try for travelers wishing to sample the diverse flavors of the nation. Aguachile is a cuisine that largely consists of fresh seafood, often shrimp or fish, marinated in a delicious and acidic sauce.

The word "aguachile" translates to "chili water" in English, which precisely defines the essence of the dish. The sauce used in aguachile is created from a blend of fresh lime juice, chili peppers (typically serrano or habanero), cilantro, garlic, and salt. These ingredients are combined together to create a zesty and spicy marinade that fills the fish with its unique flavor.

To create aguachile, the shrimp or fish is normally deveined, cleaned, and sliced into tiny pieces. It is then soaked in the marinade, allowing the flavors to enter the seafood. The acid from the lime juice essentially "cooks" the seafood, giving it a ceviche-like texture. The dish is normally served chilled, making it a refreshing option for hot summer days.

Aguachile is commonly served with accompaniments such as sliced red onions, cucumber, and avocado, which add a contrasting texture and flavor to the sour shellfish. The brilliant colors and fresh ingredients make aguachile not only a delicious dish for the taste sensations but also a feast for the eyes.

One of the best qualities of aguachile is its adaptability. While shrimp is the most usually utilized seafood, versions including fish, octopus, and even scallops can be found. Each variant delivers a unique flavor experience, as different varieties of seafood match differently with the acidic sauce.

When visiting Mexico, particularly the coastal districts, it is strongly suggested to seek out aguachile at local seafood restaurants or street food stands. The meal is a true representative of the country's culinary traditions and emphasizes the freshness of the coastal elements. Its robust flavors and refreshing properties make it a favored option among locals and visitors alike.

Churros

Churros are a popular and delectable treat that originated in Spain but have become an iconic and cherished food in Mexico as well. Churros are deep-fried sweets created from a simple dough mixture of flour, water, and salt. The dough is often piped through a star-shaped nozzle to form long, ridged strands. After frying until golden brown, churros are customarily rolled in a mixture of cinnamon and sugar, giving them a sweet and aromatic covering. They are generally served hot and fresh, making them immensely pleasant.

In Mexico, churros can be found in numerous forms and sizes. You'll come across street vendors, churrerías (churro shops), and even churro booths in major marketplaces. These eateries frequently have a colorful and pleasant environment, with the alluring aroma of churros filling the air.

One common way to eat churros in Mexico is by dipping them in a cup of thick and creamy hot chocolate. This combination offers a great mix of flavors, with the warm and crispy churros complementing the smooth and velvety chocolate. Many residents consider this combo a delicious pleasure, especially during the cooler months.

Another great variety you could discover is stuffed churros. These are churros that are piped with sweet fillings such as chocolate, caramel, or dulce de leche. The fillings provide an added layer of richness and flavor to the already exquisite dessert, making it even more enticing.

While churros can be consumed at any time of the day, they are particularly popular as a breakfast or dessert alternative. Whether you choose to taste them alongside a morning coffee or as a sweet finale to a delicious Mexican meal, churros are sure to satisfy your needs.

Churros have become a beloved part of Mexican gastronomic culture, and sampling them during your visit will offer you a full flavor of the country's culinary delicacies. Don't miss the opportunity to enjoy them as a lovely snack or a delightful treat, and don't forget to explore the numerous versions and accompaniments available.

These are only a few highlights of the huge and diverse culinary environment in Mexico. Each region has its own specialties and distinct dishes, delivering a unique gastronomic experience. Whether eating street tacos in Mexico City, reveling in Yucatecan cuisine on the Riviera Maya, or relishing seafood delights in Baja California, travelers are guaranteed to find a variety of tasty and authentic foods.

Best Time To Visit

Determining the best time to visit Mexico relies on numerous factors, including weather conditions, crowd levels, and personal tastes. Here are the many seasons and regions of Mexico to assist travelers make an informed decision about the optimal time to schedule their visit.

As noted previously, Mexico experiences a varied range of climates due to its enormous size and geographical variances. Generally, the country can be split into three primary regions: the tropical lowlands, the temperate central plateau, and the dry north. Each region has its own unique climate patterns and seasonal fluctuations.

The biggest tourist season in Mexico is during the winter months, from December through February. This period is popular with vacationers seeking warm weather and sunny skies, particularly those escaping colder climates. The coastal regions, such as Cancun, Playa del Carmen, and Los Cabos, have moderate temperatures ranging from 70°F to 85°F (21°C to 29°C) throughout this period.

However, it's crucial to realize that major tourist locations can get crowded, and prices for rooms and flights tend to be higher.

Spring (March to May) and fall (September to November) are called shoulder seasons in Mexico. During these months, the weather is often moderate, and the visitor throngs are less dense compared to winter. It's a wonderful time to visit Mexico's cultural treasures, such as ancient Mayan ruins in the Yucatan Peninsula or old colonial cities like Guanajuato and Oaxaca. Additionally, springtime offers the possibility to watch stunning natural phenomena like the migration of Monarch butterflies in Michoacán.

If you prefer to avoid enormous crowds and seek to enjoy more cheap costs, the summer months (June to August) can be an alternative for you. However, it's worth mentioning that Mexico has its rainy season around this time. The tropical lowlands and coastal regions, particularly the Gulf of Mexico and the Caribbean coast, are more prone to high rainfall and infrequent storms. On the other side, the central and northern sections of the country receive drier weather, making them perfect for exploring cities like Mexico City, Guadalajara, or Monterrey.

Another element to consider while organizing a vacation to Mexico is the existence of distinctive events and festivals. For example, the Day of the Dead celebrations in late October and early November offer a culturally immersive experience in several places, particularly in Oaxaca and Mexico City. Furthermore, the springtime provides vivid events such as Semana Santa (Holy Week) and Cinco de Mayo, which display Mexico's rich customs and heritage.

In conclusion, the best time to visit Mexico depends on your own interests, intended activities, and tolerance for crowds or specific weather conditions. The winter months offer mild weather and are perfect for beach holidays, but they tend to be more crowded and pricey. Spring and autumn give moderate weather and fewer tourists, making them perfect for cultural explorations. Summer brings lower rates but comes with the risk of rain and hurricanes, particularly in coastal places. Considering these characteristics and researching specific sites and events can help you make an informed decision and assure a pleasurable visit to Mexico, a country loaded with surprises and joys year-round.

Traveling Itinerary

Whether you have one week or two, our thorough vacation itinerary will guide you through the must-visit destinations in Mexico, ensuring an amazing experience.

1-Week Itinerary

Day 1: Arrival in Mexico City

Begin your Mexican experience in the busy capital, Mexico City. Explore the historic center, a UNESCO World Heritage site, which boasts landmarks including the Zocalo, Metropolitan Cathedral, and the National Palace. Visit the world-renowned Frida Kahlo Museum to immerse yourself in the world of Mexican art.

Day 2: Teotihuacan and Xochimilco

Embark on a day trip to Teotihuacan, an ancient Mesoamerican metropolis. Climb the Pyramid of the Sun and the Pyramid of the Moon to get panoramic views of the ruins. In the afternoon, head to Xochimilco, noted for its picturesque canals. Take a pleasant boat ride on a colorful trajinera while enjoying traditional Mexican music and food.

Day 3: Oaxaca

Fly to Oaxaca, the colonial city famed for its colorful culture and culinary delights. Explore the historic core and explore the Santo Domingo Church and Museum. Stroll through the vibrant markets and try native delicacies like tlayudas and mezcal.

Day 4: Monte Albán and Hierve el Agua

Embark on a day trip to Monte Albán, an old Zapotec archaeological site. Marvel at the stunning remains and learn about the region's rich history. Continue to Hierve el Agua, a spectacular natural beauty containing petrified waterfalls. Take a plunge in the mineral-rich waters and enjoy the spectacular views.

Day 5: Puerto Escondido

Travel to Puerto Escondido, a laid-back seaside town noted for its surfing waves. Spend the day lounging on the lovely beaches or try your hand at surfing. Explore the busy markets and savor fresh seafood at a beachfront restaurant.

Day 6: Chichen Itza

Fly to Cancun and head to Chichen Itza, one of the New Seven Wonders of the World. Admire the magnificent El Castillo pyramid and the Temple of the Warriors. Explore the sacred cenote and learn about the Mayan civilization's unique history and astronomical knowledge.

Day 7: Tulum and Playa del Carmen

Visit the beachfront village of Tulum and see its ancient Mayan ruins located on cliffs overlooking the Caribbean Sea. Relax on the gorgeous beaches and snorkel in the crystal-clear waters. In the evening, head to the vivacious town of Playa del Carmen for a taste of its exciting nightlife.

2-Week Itinerary

Days 1-7: Follow the 1-week itinerary as detailed above.

Day 8: Mérida
Travel to Mérida, the cultural hub of the Yucatan Peninsula. Explore the quaint colonial architecture, see the stunning Paseo de Montejo, and enjoy the native food, like cochinita pibil and panuchos. Don't miss the chance to experience traditional dancing and music during a lively folk performance.

Day 9: Celestun and the Pink Flamingos
Embark on a day excursion to Celestun, a coastal village famed for its natural beauty and pink flamingos. Take a boat tour through the mangroves to observe these gorgeous birds in their natural home. Enjoy the quiet beaches and eat freshly caught fish.

Day 10: Riviera Maya
Head to the Riviera Maya, a coastal paradise noted for its pristine beaches and spectacular coral reefs. Choose from a range of activities, including snorkeling, scuba diving, or simply resting on the powdered white sands. Visit the magnificent cenotes, and underground freshwater sinkholes, for a unique swimming experience.

Day 11: Cozumel
Take a ferry to the island of Cozumel, noted for its world-class diving spots. Explore the spectacular coral reefs filled with marine life, or opt for a peaceful day on the island's lovely beaches. Visit the Mayan ruins at San Gervasio and learn about the island's rich history.

Day 12: Valladolid and Ek Balam
Travel to the lovely colonial town of Valladolid, famed for its colorful streets and historical architecture. Visit the magnificent Cenote Zaci for a relaxing swim. Continue to the nearby archaeological site of Ek Balam, where you may climb

the Acropolis pyramid and enjoy panoramic views of the surrounding bush.

Day 13: Isla Holbox
Journey to the calm island of Isla Holbox, a hidden gem on Mexico's Caribbean coast. Relax on the pristine beaches, swim with whale sharks (seasonal), and enjoy the laid-back island environment. Explore the island by renting a bicycle or golf cart and eat fresh seafood at local seaside restaurants.

Day 14: Return to Mexico City
Fly back to Mexico City for your departure, but make sure to leave some time to explore the city further. Indulge in the colorful street food scene, visit world-class institutions like the National Museum of Anthropology, and buy unique souvenirs at the artisan markets.

This comprehensive vacation itinerary covers the highlights of Mexico, including classic sites like Mexico City, Teotihuacan, Oaxaca, Chichen Itza, Tulum, Mérida, Riviera Maya, Cozumel, Valladolid, Ek Balam, Isla Holbox, and more. Whether you want to spend one week or extend your stay to two, this itinerary promises a diverse and fascinating exploration of Mexico's rich past and magnificent scenery.

Visiting On a Budget

Visiting Mexico on a budget might be a fantastic choice for adventurous visitors seeking various cultural experiences, gorgeous natural scenery, and exquisite cuisine. With careful planning and wise selections, you may enjoy a fantastic trip while keeping your spending under control. Here's a complete section for travelers on a budget, covering transportation, housing, cuisine, sights, and safety precautions.

Transportation
Opting for economical transportation choices is crucial when traveling on a budget. Look for affordable flights to major Mexican cities like Mexico City, Cancun, or Guadalajara, and consider traveling during the off-peak seasons to discover the greatest rates. Alternatively, if you're already in North America, consider crossing the border by land to economize on travel.

Once in Mexico, use public transit extensively. Buses are the most prevalent and economical means of travel between cities and within metropolitan regions. Choose local buses or second-class buses, which are cheaper than luxury coaches but still give a nice trip.

Accommodation
To save money on accommodations, consider staying in budget-friendly options such as hostels, guesthouses, or budget hotels. These alternatives frequently offer clean and pleasant rooms at low rates, especially in busy tourist destinations. If you're open to more daring activities, consider camping or staying at eco-lodges in rural areas.

Food

Mexican cuisine is recognized internationally for its exquisite flavors, and you can enjoy it on a budget. Opt for local cafés, taquerías, or street food booths, where you'll find authentic and cheap cuisine. Tacos, quesadillas, tamales, and tortas are popular and budget-friendly options. Explore local markets for fresh produce and supplies to cook your own meals if you have access to a kitchenette in your hotel.

Attractions

Mexico provides a multitude of attractions that won't break the pocketbook. Take advantage of free or low-cost activities such as touring the vibrant districts of Mexico City, visiting public parks, and enjoying street entertainment. Many museums and historical sites offer cheap or free admission on specified days or during certain hours. Research these choices in advance to make the most of your stay.

Nature aficionados can enjoy Mexico's magnificent natural beauty on a budget. Visit national parks, such as Copper Canyon or Cumbres de Monterrey, where you may trek, camp, or simply absorb the stunning views. Beach enthusiasts can visit less busy coastal towns like Puerto Escondido or Tulum, which offer affordable accommodations and activities compared to more popular tourist spots.

By carefully organizing your transportation, opting for cheap hotels, eating local cuisine, discovering free or low-cost activities, and prioritizing safety, you may have a terrific journey without breaking the bank. Immerse yourself in Mexico's vibrant culture, enjoy its natural beauties, and make memorable memories without straining your budget.

Getting Around

Getting around Mexico can be a fascinating and diverse experience, as the country offers a number of transportation options to suit different interests and budgets. From bustling cities to quiet beach communities and historic archaeological sites, Mexico has something for everyone.

Air travel is still the popular and convenient option to cross big distances within Mexico. The country has many international airports, including Mexico City International Airport, Cancún International Airport, and Guadalajara International Airport, which serve as significant hubs for local and international flights. From these airports, tourists can easily connect to many places within the country.

For shorter distances or commuting inside a certain region, buses are an excellent option. Mexico provides a vast network of bus services, ranging from elegant coaches to inexpensive local buses. Companies like ADO, ETN, and Primera Plus offer pleasant, air-conditioned buses with reclining seats, onboard facilities, and occasionally even Wi-Fi. These buses normally operate on set timetables and serve both big cities and smaller communities.

Railway is also another common mode of transportation in Mexico. Although the railroad network is not as vast as in some other nations, it offers scenic journeys and an opportunity to visit particular regions. The most famous railroad route in Mexico is the Chihuahua al Pacífico, better known as the Copper Canyon Railway, which goes through the magnificent Copper Canyon in the northwest.

In major regions, such as Mexico City, Guadalajara, and Monterrey, public transportation options include the metro, buses, and taxis. The Mexico City Metro is the largest and busiest metro system in Latin America, with various lines linking different regions of the city. Buses are an economical and commonly available means of transportation, although they can be crowded and vulnerable to traffic congestion. Taxis are also prevalent, and it is encouraged to use approved taxis or ride-hailing services for safety and reliability.

For those seeking more flexibility, renting a car is a popular choice. Renting a car in Mexico allows vacationers to explore at their own leisure and see off-the-beaten-path sites. Major vehicle rental firms have branches at airports and in major cities. However, it's vital to understand that driving in Mexico can be tough, especially in busy places or unfamiliar country roads. It is advisable to familiarize oneself with local traffic laws and use caution.

In coastal districts and famous tourist attractions, such as Cancún, Playa del Carmen, and Puerto Vallarta, water transportation is often accessible. Ferry services run between mainland Mexico and tourist islands, such as Cozumel and Isla Mujeres. Additionally, boat trips and water taxis give transportation to scenic areas, such as secret beaches and snorkeling sites.

When it comes to safety, it's crucial for travelers to be vigilant and take the required precautions while traveling around Mexico. It is advisable to examine the safety status in certain places, follow local advice, and avoid traveling at night in unknown or high-risk areas. It's also essential to keep important documents, such as passports and IDs, secure and maintain a backup copy.

Whether traveling within a region or crossing longer distances, travelers may navigate Mexico easily and comfortably. By being aware of safety risks and planning beforehand, travelers can have a memorable and pleasurable experience exploring all that Mexico has to offer.

Shopping for Souvenirs

Mexico also offers an astounding range of souvenirs for travelers to take home as cherished recollections. From traditional handicrafts to modern artworks, Mexico's marketplaces and shops are filled with unique items that represent the country's diverse background. Here's an overview of Mexico's souvenir-buying scene, including famous shopping areas, must-buy items, negotiating advice, and cultural etiquette. Whether you're strolling through crowded markets or visiting elegant boutiques, this section will help you navigate the shopping experience and ensure you locate the ideal mementos to recall your time in Mexico.

Exploring Popular Shopping Destinations

Mexico provides a number of attractive shopping places that cater to every taste and budget. Here are some of the must-visit sites for souvenir shopping:

Mercado de Artesanias La Ciudadela (Mexico City): Located in the center of Mexico City, La Ciudadela is a treasure trove of Mexican handicrafts. The market offers a broad assortment of commodities like ceramics, textiles, silver jewelry, leather goods, and traditional attire.

Mercado 28 (Cancun): This bustling open-air market in Cancun is noted for its bright ambiance and varied choice of merchandise. Here, you can discover anything from bright sombreros and hand-painted ceramics to Mayan-inspired jewelry and hammocks.

San Juan Market (Mexico City): Food lovers and culinary connoisseurs will delight in exploring the San Juan Market. This gourmet market is the ideal spot to pick up unique cuisine items such as chile sauces, Mexican spices, artisanal chocolates, and traditional sweets.

Must-Buy Souvenirs

Mexico provides a choice of classic mementos that encapsulate the essence of its rich cultural heritage. Here are some must-buy goods to consider:

Talavera Pottery: Hailing from Puebla, Talavera Pottery is recognized for its bright hand-painted motifs. From beautiful plates and vases to tiles and kitchenware, Talavera pottery offers a bit of Mexican flair to any house.

Textiles: Mexico's textiles are a monument to the country's indigenous heritage. Look for intricately woven textiles, including blankets, carpets, shawls, and embroidered clothes, which represent the rich colors and patterns distinctive to diverse areas.

Alebrijes: These whimsical, hand-carved wooden sculptures originate from the state of Oaxaca. Crafted in intricate detail, alebrijes portray fanciful creatures and animals, making them an appealing and eye-catching keepsake.

Lucha Libre Masks: Lucha Libre, Mexican professional wrestling, is a prominent cultural phenomenon. Capture the atmosphere of this theatrical sport by obtaining an authentic Lucha Libre mask, a bright and unusual keepsake.

Bargaining Tips and Cultural Etiquette

Bargaining is a prevalent activity in Mexican markets and small shops. Here are some guidelines to assist you negotiate the bargaining process and achieve a fair deal:

Polite Negotiation: Approach bargaining with a polite and respectful attitude. Engage in cordial conversation with the dealer and exhibit genuine interest in their items.

Comparison Shopping: Before settling on a price, visit various stores or stalls to get an idea of the average price range for the item you're interested in. This will provide you leverage during negotiations and help you make an informed decision.

Start Low: Begin the bargaining process by providing a price much lower than the initial asking price. This offers flexibility for discussion and gives the vendor an opportunity to counteroffer.

Maintain a Budget: Determine the maximum amount you're willing to pay for an item and adhere to it. Avoid getting caught up in the excitement of haggling and overspending.

Bundle Purchases: Consider purchasing many things from the same merchant. This provides you greater leverage to negotiate better overall pricing for the bundle.

Respect Cultural Etiquette: It's crucial to be cognizant of the local culture and customs while bargaining. Maintain a respectful tone and avoid becoming angry or hostile during discussions.

Politeness and Gratitude: Regardless of the outcome, always thank the vendor for their time and concern. Even if you don't achieve an agreement, departing on a pleasant note can generate a lasting impression.

Authenticity and Fair Trade

When shopping for souvenirs in Mexico, it's crucial to support local craftsmen and choose real, fair-trade products. Look for certifications such as "Hecho en México" (Made in Mexico) or "Artesanía Mexicana" (Mexican Handcraft) to confirm the authenticity and quality of your products.

By supporting local artists and fair-trade practices, you contribute to the preservation of traditional workmanship and help sustain local economies. Additionally, buying directly from artisans or recognized cooperatives guarantees that they earn a fair amount of profits for their hard work.

Remember that true Mexican handicraft may be priced higher than mass-produced imitations, but the quality and cultural value they symbolize are worth the expenditure. Ask sellers about the materials used and the process involved in manufacturing the items to obtain a deeper appreciation for the craftsmanship.

Conclusion

Shopping for gifts in Mexico is a fascinating experience that allows you to immerse yourself in the country's rich culture and support local artists. By touring famous shopping destinations, understanding must-buy items, refining your bargaining abilities, and observing cultural etiquette, you can make informed and meaningful purchases. Remember to favor authenticity and fair-trade principles, since this ensures that your mementos carry the real character of Mexico while benefiting the local people. So, begin your shopping expedition with an open mind and embrace the delight of finding unique things that will forever remember your journey through Mexico's beautiful tapestry of art, history, and culture.

Tour Package Options

Whether you're interested in discovering ancient ruins, lounging on pristine beaches, immersing yourself in rich cultural traditions, or indulging in excellent cuisine, Mexico has something to offer for every sort of tourist. Here are the numerous tour package options available in Mexico:

Historical and Cultural Tours: Mexico is home to various archaeological sites and historical landmarks. Tour packages concentrating on the country's rich history and culture generally include excursions to prominent sites including Chichen Itza, Teotihuacan, and Palenque. These trips provide insights into the ancient civilizations of the Mayans and Aztecs, allowing travelers to explore awe-inspiring ruins and learn about the country's pre-Columbian origins.

Beach and Resort Packages: Mexico features some of the most gorgeous beaches in the world. Tourists seeking relaxation and sun-soaked vacations can choose from a choice of beach and resort packages. Popular destinations include Cancun, Playa del Carmen, and Tulum on the Caribbean coast, as well as Los Cabos and Puerto Vallarta on the Pacific coast. These packages frequently include accommodation at upscale beachside resorts, access to water sports activities, and possibilities for leisurely beach hopping.

Eco-Tours & Nature Exploration: Mexico's natural beauty extends beyond its beaches. The country is blessed with various ecosystems, including lush jungles, pure cenotes (natural sinkholes), and gorgeous national parks. Eco-tour programs give possibilities for trekking, wildlife viewing, snorkeling in crystal-clear cenotes, and visiting hidden jewels like the Sian Ka'an Biosphere Reserve and Copper Canyon. These tours give an intimate experience of Mexico's distinctive flora and fauna.

Culinary Experiences: Mexican cuisine is famous worldwide for its richness and variety. Food aficionados might select travel packages that focus on culinary activities. These packages generally include excursions to local markets, cooking workshops, and food-tasting tours. Travelers may sample traditional delicacies like tacos, mole, and ceviche, while also learning about the cultural significance of each culinary creation.

Adventure and Outdoor Activities: For adrenaline seekers and outdoor enthusiasts, Mexico provides thrilling adventure tour packages. From zip-lining beneath verdant canopies to exploring underground rivers in cenotes, there is no shortage of interesting activities. Popular adventure sites include the Riviera Maya, where travelers can go snorkeling, scuba diving, or cave diving in the famous cenotes. Additionally, the Copper Canyon offers options for hiking, biking, and zip-lining amidst stunning canyons.

City Tours: Mexico's lively cities are loaded with history, art, and distinct cultural experiences. City trip packages generally include excursions to Mexico City, Guadalajara, and Oaxaca, where tourists may explore colonial architecture, visit world-class museums, and indulge in traditional festivities. These tours provide insights into Mexico's contemporary culture and urban lifestyle.

From seeing ancient ruins to lazing on pristine beaches, from relishing excellent cuisine to indulging in exhilarating adventures, there is something for everyone. Whether you're a history buff, nature lover, gourmet enthusiast, or adventure seeker, Mexico's numerous offers promise an amazing encounter.

Tourist Safety Tips

While it offers stunning vistas, rich cultural heritage, and exquisite cuisine, it is necessary for visitors to consider their safety. By following several important principles, travelers can have a safe and pleasurable stay in Mexico.

Research and Planning
Before leaving on your journey, careful research and planning are vital. Understand the regions you plan to visit, particularly their current safety circumstances. Stay updated on travel advisories published by your government, as well as information from credible sources such as tourism boards and consulates. Choose trustworthy hotel alternatives and transportation providers, and consider travel insurance that covers medical emergencies and trip cancellations.

Transportation Safety
When traveling within Mexico, it is advised to use registered taxis or ride-sharing services rather than catching random cabs. Avoid taking rides from strangers. If renting a car, choose a trusted agency and check the vehicle is in good shape. Stick to well-lit, crowded areas, and be aware of excessive speeding or dangerous driving. It is also advised to avoid traveling at night whenever feasible.

Personal Security
Maintaining personal security is crucial. Avoid displaying precious objects openly, such as expensive jewelry or significant sums of cash. Use a money belt or a disguised bag to secure your money and vital documents. Stay in well-populated locations, particularly at night, and alert someone about your route.

Public Safety Awareness

Being aware of your surroundings and using caution in public settings is vital. Be aware of busy areas, as they may attract pickpockets or other petty thieves. Keep a tight eye on your belongings and avoid leaving them unattended. It is advisable to avoid flashing evidence of luxury or bringing unwanted attention to yourself. If you see a demonstration or protest, remain aside and choose an alternate route to guarantee your safety.

Respect the Local Laws and Customs

Respect for local laws and customs is crucial in any foreign place, and Mexico is no exception. Familiarize yourself with the local customs, traditions, and laws of the locations you plan to visit. Dress correctly, be cognizant of cultural conventions, and abide by local legislation. Avoid engaging in unlawful activities, including drug-related offenses, as the repercussions might be severe.

Conclusion

Traveling to Mexico may be a fantastic experience, and by prioritizing safety, travelers can fully appreciate all that the nation has to offer. A thorough study, preparation, and staying informed are vital. Taking care of transportation, personal security, and public safety knowledge can dramatically lessen potential threats. Respecting local laws and customs is equally vital for a happy and safe travel experience. By following this detailed safety advice, travelers may make the most of their visit to Mexico while protecting their well-being throughout their stay.

Festival and Events

Mexico is also recognized for its colorful festivals and events that captivate locals and tourists alike. From colorful holidays steeped in ancient customs to current cultural extravaganzas, the Mexican calendar is replete with an array of engaging activities. Here are some of Mexico's festivals and events, giving light to their historical significance, cultural value, and the unique experiences they offer to guests.

Day of the Dead

Undoubtedly one of Mexico's most recognizable celebrations, the Day of the Dead is a deeply ingrained tradition that commemorates and celebrates deceased loved ones. Held annually from October 31st to November 2nd, this colorful and happy event incorporates ornate altars, sugar skulls, marigolds, and parades. Visitors can immerse themselves in the colorful ambiance of cemeteries, where families congregate to honor their relatives or see enthralling street processions. The festival displays Mexico's profound reverence for death as a natural part of life and offers a unique cultural glimpse into the country's indigenous heritage.

Guelaguetza Festival

Originating from the Zapotec and Mixtec cultures of Oaxaca, the Guelaguetza Festival is a beautiful showcase of traditional music, dance, and regional costumes. Taking place in July, this week-long festival showcases the different ethnic communities in the region, each presenting their particular cultural performances. Visitors can witness stunning dance routines, sample local cuisine, and visit the bustling arts and crafts market. The Guelaguetza Festival is a monument to

Mexico's rich indigenous heritage and acts as a platform for conserving and promoting the country's traditional customs.

Cervantino International Festival

Named after Miguel de Cervantes, the renowned Spanish author of "Don Quixote," the Cervantino International Festival is a celebration of the arts held yearly in Guanajuato. With its origins reaching back to 1972, this famous event has become one of the most prominent cultural festivals in Latin America. Over the course of three weeks in October, the city is transformed into a hive of theatrical productions, music concerts, dance acts, and art exhibitions. The Cervantino Festival invites renowned performers from throughout the world, creating a unique cultural blend that mesmerizes audiences.

Feria Nacional de San Marcos

Known as the "San Marcos Fair," this historical festival is hosted in the city of Aguascalientes during the month of April. Combining traditional festivals with modern attractions, the fair offers a genuinely immersive experience for guests of all ages. From spectacular bullfights and equestrian shows to live music concerts and amusement park rides, the Feria Nacional de San Marcos has something for everyone. This colorful event is strongly established in Mexican culture and highlights the country's enthusiasm for entertainment, agriculture, and folklore.

Conclusion

Mexico's festivals and events offer a peek into the country's rich tapestry of cultural heritage and traditions. From the profound reverence of the Day of the Dead to the colorful energy of the Guelaguetza Festival, each event provides a unique look into Mexico's different cultures and historical heritage. Whether you prefer to observe ancient traditions or bask in contemporary artistic manifestations, these festivals offer an immersive and fascinating experience for travelers. So, pack your bags, embrace the passion of Mexico, and embark on a journey packed with colors, cuisines, and beautiful events.

Conclusion

From the bustling streets of Mexico City to the tranquil beaches of Cancún, we have explored the country's diverse landscapes, rich history, vibrant culture, and exquisite cuisine. Throughout our research, we have realized that Mexico genuinely has something for everyone, whether you're an adventure seeker, a history buff, a nature lover, or a foodie.

One of the most stunning elements of Mexico is its incredible natural beauty. From the awe-inspiring Copper Canyon in Chihuahua to the pristine beaches of the Riviera Maya, the country provides a broad spectrum of landscapes that will leave any traveler in wonder. Whether you're hiking through lush jungles, swimming in crystal-clear cenotes, or marveling at the sight of migrating whales off the Baja California coast, Mexico offers many possibilities to connect with nature and create unique experiences.

Beyond its natural charms, Mexico is immersed in a rich and ancient history that can be felt in every corner of the country. The relics of spectacular ancient civilizations such as the Mayans, Aztecs, and Olmecs are dispersed throughout Mexico, with prominent monuments like Chichén Itzá, Teotihuacán, and Palenque standing as testaments to their grandeur. Exploring these archaeological wonders allows us to understand the riddles of the past and develop a deeper appreciation for the creativity and artistry of these ancient societies.

The cultural heritage of Mexico is as diverse as its landscape. From vivid festivals and traditional dances to colorful handicrafts and detailed artwork, Mexico's culture is a tapestry woven with indigenous roots and colonial influences. Cities like Oaxaca, Guanajuato, and San Miguel de Allende are treasure troves for art connoisseurs, offering a glimpse into Mexico's dynamic art scene. Meanwhile, the Day of the Dead celebrations in areas like Mexico City and Mérida provides a unique and immersive experience, commemorating the country's ancestral traditions.

No travel guide to Mexico would be complete without addressing the wonderful flavors of Mexican gastronomy. From the aromatic spices of the mole to the acidic freshness of ceviche, Mexican food is a gourmet joy that caters to all tastes. Whether you're indulging in street tacos, relishing a traditional mole poblano, or experiencing regional delicacies like cochinita pibil or chiles en nogada, Mexico's gastronomy is a sensory experience that will leave you hungry for more.

As we complete our Mexico Travel Guide, it's vital to stress that Mexico is a country that goes beyond the clichés typically depicted in the media. While there are clearly locations that require caution and awareness, the vast majority of Mexico is a safe and inviting destination for travelers. By applying common sense, respecting local customs, and embracing the warmth of the Mexican people, you can uncover a world of unique experiences and create cherished memories that will last a lifetime.

Whether you're planning a single adventure, a romantic retreat, or a family holiday, Mexico has it all. Its natural marvels, ancient history, colorful culture, and excellent food make it a very compelling destination. So pack your bags, immerse yourself in the brilliant colors, sounds, and flavors of Mexico, and let this travel book be your companion as you start on a memorable adventure through one of the most compelling countries in the world. Viva México!

Printed in Great Britain
by Amazon

32894415R00089